CW00376024

EQUAL **Success Stories**

Development Partnerships
working against discrimination and inequality
in Europe

Free Movement of Good Ideas

Employment & social affairs

European Commission
Directorate-General for Employment, Social Affairs
and Equal Opportunities
Unit B.4
Manuscript completed in September 2005

The contents of this publication do not necessarily reflect the opinion or position of the European Commission, Directorate-General for Employment, Social Affairs and Equal Opportunities.

If you are interested in receiving the electronic newsletter "ESmail" from the European Commission's Directorate-General for Employment, Social Affairs and Equal Opportunities, please send an e-mail to empl-esmail@cec.eu.int. The newsletter is published on a regular basis in English, French and German.

**Europe Direct is a service to help you find answers
to your questions about the European Union**

Freephone number:
00 800 6 7 8 9 10 11

A great deal of additional information on the European Union is available on the Internet. It can be accessed through the Europa server (http://europa.eu.int).

Cataloguing data can be found at the end of this publication.

Luxembourg: Office for Official Publications of the European Communities, 2005

ISBN 92-79-00180-9

Foreword

You are about to read a series of success stories developed within the European Commission's EQUAL programme.

This European Social Fund Initiative aims to overcome discrimination in the workplace and in accessing employment – a key element of the European Union's strategy to create more and better jobs. By promoting a more inclusive labour market, the EU can increase participation in employment and learning, and maximise the contribution of every individual to the economy and society as a whole.

The EQUAL Initiative, launched in 2000, is designed to investigate and test different ways of tackling discrimination in employment and on the job market and to share examples of the resulting good practice across borders, with the intention of influencing policy and general practice throughout Europe.

EQUAL is jointly financed by the European Social Fund and the Member States and is structured around six key principles, or "building blocks": Innovation, Partnership, Empowerment, Transnational cooperation, Thematic focus and Mainstreaming. Although the two rounds of EQUAL projects have already been selected (in 2001 and 2004), Development Partnerships will still be actively implementing their work programmes up to 2008.

Harvesting the results of the first round of projects is at the heart of this publication. But these are just some of the activities implemented and tested at local, regional or national level. Several national and transnational networks are constantly seeking out the best practices and most innovative elements of EQUAL's work to make sure others can benefit from the lessons learned. Besides the success stories featured in this publication, a myriad of other examples and results can be found on the European Commission's EQUAL website (http://europa.eu.int/comm/employment_social/equal) and the different national EQUAL sites.

The EQUAL projects presented in this publication offer just a few examples of best practice. They are organised by theme, and each story includes an index to show which of the different EQUAL principles are best illustrated by the project. You can find a short explanation of the principles and an overview of the projects presented in the tables overleaf.

Each of these projects has made its own unique and important contribution to overcoming discrimination in Europe. They give just a glimpse of what can be achieved through committed partnerships working together towards a common goal. We hope they will provide inspiration and new ideas on how to apply the lessons learnt more widely across Europe.

Happy reading!

Principles

The EQUAL Development Partnerships are built on six underlying principles. The examples selected illustrate how one or more of these principles are applied in practice.

Partnership: Bringing together key actors in Development Partnerships (DPs) on a geographical or sectoral level to tackle discrimination and inequality

Empowerment: Strengthening the capacity of all stakeholders, including beneficiaries, by working together on an equal footing

Transnational cooperation: Learning from experiences in other Member States, transferring good practice from one region to another, and establishing durable networks

Innovation: Developing and testing new approaches

Mainstreaming: Sharing good practice and influencing policies and practice

Thematic focus: Concentrating on a thematic field consistent with the European Employment Strategy (see below).

Thematic focus

Many experimental activities cover several different issues. But they can be clustered under the following general themes:

Employability: access and return to the labour market, diversity, pathways to employment, education and training

Entrepreneurship: business support, micro-finance, social enterprise

Adaptability: lifelong learning, age management, ICT & knowledge society

Equal opportunities: participation of women, work-life balance, desegregation

Asylum seekers: social integration.

Contents

Valuing Carers

Some six million people in the UK are carers for partners, relatives or friends who are ill, frail or have a disability. But juggling care responsibilities with paid employment can be difficult, and many people are forced to change the way the work or to give up work altogether. This can create more problems – many carers see their incomes plummet, they become socially isolated, their work skills become out of date and all this can lead to low self-esteem.

Thanks to an EQUAL Development Partnership (DP) called Action for Carers and Employment (ACE National), the difficulties carers face in the job market are now widely recognised and are being addressed by employers, training providers, other service providers and politicians.

Validating and strengthening existing skills

One of the legacies of this DP, for example, is the "Learning for Living" qualification and learning resource. Developed by City & Guilds, a DP partner, this on-line learning programme helps users identify and build on their existing skills, and work towards a nationally recognised qualification known as the "Certificate in Personal Development and Learning for Unpaid Carers". The course has been of real benefit to individuals in terms of building self-confidence and restoring self-esteem. As one participant, who had to give up work to care for her brother, said: "...the learning for living course made me realise that I have a lot to offer".

ACE National also focused on raising the awareness of carers' needs among those working in different public services, such as health, social care, education, employment services and the voluntary sector. For example, a "Carer Awareness Training Programme" has been adapted from a course trialed by one of the DP's local partners, Action For Carers in Surrey. And a training pack entitled "Young Carers and the Connexions Service" aims to sensitise professionals providing career guidance to young people on the specific needs and problems faced by young carers.

To ensure that the EQUAL project formulate its policy recommendations on solid foundations, two important research studies were carried out. A study into the real value of carers' support concluded that carers in fact save the UK economy a staggering £57 billion (€ 83 billion) each year – the equivalent of a second National Health Service (the report "Without Us" is available via the DPs website). The conclusions of a second study on barriers and bridges for carers in employment are published in a report entitled "Redressing the Balance".

Employers – the most effective advocates

Crucial to the DP's overall success was the direct involvement of public and private employers such as government departments and major companies, as well as the social partners represented by the Confederation of British Industry and three trade unions. Major UK employers, such as British Telecom or PricewaterhouseCoopers, have now become among the most vocal advocates of the DP's message – that employing carers makes good business sense. With secretarial and administrative support from ACE, these and other influential employers have created and now operate the Employers for Carers interest group (www.employersforcarers.org.uk). The website provides guidance to employers on how to help carers continue to work, and to attract additional carers into their companies.

But a key objective of ACE National was to ensure that the good practices developed and lessons learnt become integrated into mainstream policy and programmes. And its efforts have certainly paid off. ACE helped to steer a Private Members Bill on providing more recognition and equality of opportunities to carers through the UK Parliament. The Carers (Equal Opportunities) Act received Royal Assent in July 2004. It places new duties on local authorities to ensure that carers have access to employment, education and leisure opportunities – the first time that these key issues for carers have been addressed in the context of equal opportunities and diversity. According to the Member of Parliament responsible for introducing the bill, Dr Hywel Francis, "ACE National's innovative partnership saw the Carers (Equal Opportunities) Act through all its stages in Parliament, giving it support from a whole range of key stakeholders, from individual carers to major employers."

Another interesting outcome of the DP's activities is the Carers Award category in the Employer of the Year Awards. Run by Working Families, a leading charity in the field of work-life balance, these awards promote innovative employment policies which support people to manage work and external responsibilities (www.workingfam-

Lord Pendry, Dr Hywel Francis MP and Malcolm Wicks MP, Minister of State for Energy, who all successfully took the Carers Act through Parliament

ilies.org.uk). In 2004, the award was won by a member of the Employers for Carers group, the Department for Constitutional Affairs, which acknowledged at the time that "*we would not have achieved this success without the support of ACE.*"

Key factors for success

The DP's success in achieving long-term positive changes to policy and practice can be attributed to several key factors. Firstly, Carers UK, the lead partner has a strong track record in lobbying and campaigning, strong parliamentary links, a wide membership and a dedicated training unit. Secondly, the partnership between local partners – that developed and tested new tools, plus national partners – that could transfer this experience nationwide, was particularly effective. The partners also took every opportunity to publicise the DPs message, "piggybacking" on many existing and new campaigns. Finally, the emphasis on involving the media, organising events in prestigious surroundings and inviting Government Ministers to sponsor and chair events, added to the DP's public profile.

> "*Without EQUAL and the attention and resources that it devotes to effective partnership and mainstreaming activities, we would never have been in a position to push, or to help other people push, for these very positive changes in the UK Government's policies!*" Madeleine Starr, Coordinator of ACE National.

A new EQUAL project "ACE 2" is now underway. Building on the success of its predecessor, this DP will be working towards the establishment of a National Care Strategy.

A more detailed version and other EQUAL success stories can be found at: http://europa.eu.int/comm/employment_social/equal/activities/search_en.cfm

Country: United Kingdom
Region: National
Project name: ACE National
Project duration: November 2001 – November 2005
ESF priority area: Employability
ESF funding (€): 2 543 035
Total funding (€): 7 489 662
National EQUAL partners:
18 national partners
Transnational partnership with: Austria
Contact details:
ACE National
Ms Madeleine Starr
Carers UK
20-25 Glasshouse Yard
GB-London EC1A 4JT
Tel: +44 20 7566 7607
E-mail: madeleine.starr@carersuk.org
Website: www.carersuk.org.uk

Innovation ▶

Mainstreaming ▶

Transnationality

Empowerment

Partnership

Encouraging and understanding diversity

Situated in West Yorkshire, Kirklees is the seventh largest metropolitan district in the United Kingdom. The availability of work in the 1950s and 1960s attracted many immigrant workers and today 14% of the population is from a minority ethnic background – well above the UK average of 9%. However, wage levels are below the national average, with 25% of local jobs in manufacturing.

This EQUAL Development Partnership (DP) has established "Common Ground" with employers, promoting the principle that diversity pays and that by identifying and building on the latent skills of the population, it is possible to move towards a more productive local economy and a more inclusive society.

A laboratory for new approaches

Common Ground has had a significant impact at local level. Nearly 900 individuals and over 100 businesses have benefited from the wide range of support available through the DP and over 60 people gained employment, while 85 jobs were safeguarded. In effect, Common Ground has been a vast laboratory in which a host of different approaches to labour market integration have been tried and tested.

The EQUAL project was created after a process of widespread consultation that resulted in 21 organisations signing up to become members. They include voluntary organisations, community groups, the public employment service, the Learning and Skills Council and the local Chamber of Commerce.

To manage the diverse partners and approaches, the DP set up two overarching frameworks for its activities. The first, a Mentoring Network, ensures that the coaching and

"*The Common Ground Development Partnership was especially interested in working with employers to break down stereotypes and preconceptions and to promote processes and structures to support diversity in the workplace,*" says Jennifer Reeves of Business Link West Yorkshire, one of the strategic partners in project. "*It took a lot of hard work but Common Ground has really succeeded in harnessing the hidden potential of our people in Kirklees.*"

support offered to all target groups is of a similar standard and that lessons learned with each group are disseminated and built into future approaches and procedures. The Network includes six pilot projects with a mentoring dimension.

Career support and coaching

Mehnaz Dad has been working with the Mentoring Network for six months and has been trained to provide support, guidance and assistance to mentees in their search for further training or employment. "*The training I have received has made a big impact on my life. Mentoring has given me the confidence to approach people and use my listening skills to help them. It has also helped me to progress further in my career, into another field of employment, with the Community Mental Health Team.*"

The second DP network was built on an earlier employers' network and has led to the creation of the "Equality at Work" Award. The target group is smaller businesses,

which are often confused about equality-related employment legislation and lack dedicated human resource or equality specialists. The award challenges the views of some employers that equality-related measures can act as a burden.

Andy Aldridge is the Managing Director of one of the 30 small businesses to have received the award: "*The biggest business benefit has been the improved image of our organisation. We are now much more reflective of our local society and potential customer base. As a result, it has helped us develop new markets and business opportunities and enabled us to recruit from groups who may not previously have joined our company.*"

One of the DP's 12 innovations – the Equaliser project connecting with "hard to reach" young people

Promoting equality policies at work

The Partnership has also produced a variety of user-friendly products and toolkits for employers including a Disability Discrimination Toolkit, a Work-Life Balance Toolkit, a Mentor Training Pack and an Employment Good Practice Guide specifically designed for voluntary sector employers.

A new EQUAL project is now coming on stream called "Common Ground – Breaking New Ground". Through her experience of managing the first EQUAL DP and providing the secretariat for the transnational partnership "Diverse Reflections", Heather Waddington emphasises the added value of working across borders: "*transnational activities will bring novel ideas and innovative approaches to help us break new ground in Kirklees. We are excited about working with this next set of European partners and hope that our cooperation will be as productive and enjoyable as it has been in Diverse Reflections.*"

A more detailed version and other EQUAL success stories can be found at: http://europa.eu.int/comm/employment_social/equal/activities/search_en.cfm

Country: United Kingdom
Region: Yorkshire & Humberside
Project name: Common Ground
Project duration: November 2001 – November 2005
ESF priority area: Employability
ESF funding (€): 2 240 471
Total funding (€): 6 586 988
National EQUAL partners: Kirklees Metropolitan Council and twelve partners
Transnational partnership with: Denmark, the Netherlands, Germany
Contact details:
European Unit
Economic Development Services
Ms Heather Waddington
Civic Centre III
GB-Huddersfield HD1 2EY
Tel: +44 1484 221416
E-mail: heather.waddington@kirklees.gov.uk
Website: www.diverse-reflections.com

Innovation ►

Mainstreaming

Transnationality

Empowerment ►

Partnership ►

Changing perceptions of immigration: from threat to opportunity

The number of foreign residents in Upper Austria has grown by 40% since the early 1990s, now representing more than 7% of the region's population. The most significant immigrant groups come from Ex-Yugoslavia (53%) and Turkey (17%). Against this background, the eastern enlargement of the EU and the dismantling of the border with the Czech Republic have fermented fears among the population about a new wave of immigration.

"We need to stimulate a sustainable process of reflection upon these issues. Fear is a poor adviser. We must remove the frontiers that exist in the people's minds. This is why information and raising awareness of the general public are the core activities of the project" said Alfred Obermüller, a Member of Parliament, at a press conference that outlined the ambitions of the Living and Working Together Development Partnership (DP). Under the overall management of the regional branch of the Trade Union Federation (ÖGB) in Linz, this project has been one of the few EQUAL projects where a trade union has taken the lead role.

Putting unjustified fears into perspective

Living and Working Together launched a well-targeted and diversified information campaign to convince the population a change in attitudes to migrants and minorities was essential both for the economic development and social inclusiveness of the region. It consisted of three distinct but mutually reinforcing actions to raise the public's awareness about xenophobia and racism and to promote the empowerment of minorities. These actions generated considerable interest from local and regional media.

> *"Before we began our work in the DP, such positive reporting about our Czech neighbours was unimaginable. Our programme has clearly helped to put into perspective many wrong perceptions and unjustified fears."* Gabriele Lackner-Strauss, Chair of the Chamber of Employers in Freistadt.

Firstly, regional development was promoted as one of the benefits of a cross-border labour market. Though EU enlargement was opening up new perspectives for change and growth, employers and their workforces were very sceptical about these opportunities, mainly because they were not yet familiar with strategies for cross-border regional development. The DP launched a comprehensive programme of information seminars and workshops together with a successful mobile exhibition. The programme addressed employers and employees, those responsible for labour market policy and local decision makers. It stimulated debate on the opportunities emerging from the eastern enlargement, on issues related to "new migration" and on the integration of "traditional" migrants and minorities. In addition, Local Community Dialogue events brought together members of municipal councils, mayors, local associations and multipliers and a bi-lingual regional information platform was developed that continues to be accessible via the internet.

Reporting racism and supporting victims

Secondly, a central Anti-Racism Contact Point (ARAS) with five local branches was set up by one of the NGO partners in the DP to identify, document and follow up racist/xenophobic incidents. The service offers legal information, advice and a multi-stage process of practical support to victims of racism. A regional Advisory Council has also been established, in cooperation with the police, to provide guidance on how to follow up cases reported, and a series of 20 anti-racism workshops were organised.

Thirdly, the Trade Union Federation piloted a model for a new type of intercultural training course which involves the paired participation of shop stewards and fellow workers from migrant or minority origin.

An opportunity, not a threat

There is now a more open attitude towards cross-frontier cooperation amongst employers in the border area and especially amongst SMEs, and a much stronger interest in exploring the potential of the new market. *"Initially, I saw enlargement as a threat. I was afraid of the new, and possibly fierce, competition and felt that the government should do more to protect domestic companies. I now realise that we must adapt to the new situation and I now know how I can do that. The opening of the labour market has provided new opportunities to develop our business, together with Czech partners. My first contact with them has shown me that they face problems that are very similar to ours,"* said Walter, who runs a small transport firm.

The DP brought together a partnership of nine key regional actors concerned that negative attitudes to immigration would hamper the region's capacity to tap into the new opportunities emerging from the opening of the labour market.

Government involvement lent weight

The first step in confronting this challenge was the creation of a common platform for planning and action that involved all the relevant stakeholders, including both operators in the field and the strategic partners. This structure and the direct involvement of the regional government gave the DP greater recognition and, in turn, stimulated the accountability and commitment of the individual partners. It also helped in the allocation of clear and distinct responsibilities and in ensuring that these were respected. The cooperative working and information processes within the Partnership created a climate of mutual trust helping to demonstrate good practice and achieve effective outcomes.

Strategic partners, who include the Chamber of Employers, the Chamber of Workers, the regional Government and relevant NGOs, provided advice and policy support in the design, coordination and development of all actions. Perhaps more importantly, they are also helping to ensure that most of the activities piloted by Living and Working Together will be continued as part of mainstream programmes in Upper Austria.

A more detailed version and other EQUAL success stories can be found at: http://europa.eu.int/comm/employment_social/equal/activities/ search_en.cfm

Country: Austria
Region: Upper Austria
Project name: Miteinander arbeiten und leben (Living and working together)
Project duration: September 2002 – September 2005
ESF priority area: Employability
ESF funding (€): 912 826
Total funding (€): 1 825 652
National EQUAL partners: Amt der Oberösterreichischen Landesregierung – Sozialabteilung, Arbeiterkammer Oberösterreich, EUREGIO – Bayerischer Wald – Böhmerwald – Regionalmanagement Mühlviertel, Institut für Soziologie – Uni Linz, Land der Menschen – Aufeinander zugehen Oberösterreich, Verein Mauthausen Komitee Österreich, Verein zur Betreuung der AusländerInnen in Oberösterreich, Wirtschaftskammer Oberösterreich
Transnational partnership with: Germany, Italy
Contact details:
ÖGB Oberösterreich – EU Projektbüro
Heinrich Wenidoppler
Güntherstraße 1
A-4040 Linz
Tel: +43 732 737 187-11
E-mail: gabriela.maurer@aan.at
website: www.miteinanderundleben.at

Innovation ▶

Mainstreaming

Transnationality

Empowerment ▶

Partnership

Tapping the employment potential of SMEs

The Flemish labour market is marked by two particular problems – the relatively low number of older people in employment and the high jobless rate among migrants. In 2003, only 42.4% of those aged 50-64 were in work, compared to 52.9% for the EU-15 as a whole. Meanwhile, the unemployment rate for non-EU nationals resident in Belgium was 25.3%, compared to 4.5% for those with Belgian nationality.

Tackling these issues is therefore driving the Flemish Government's diversity policy. Its main priorities are to encourage cooperation between sectors, invest in the social economy to create subsidised jobs, promote equal opportunity policies and support organisations in developing their own diversity policies. In the case of migrants, there is also a political will to ensure proportional labour market participation by 2010, so that their rates of employment reflect the percentage of the population that they represent.

A personal approach to small businesses

The Paradox Development Partnership (DP) is unique in Belgium as it exclusively targets SMEs to realise its main objective of increasing the employment rates of older people and migrants. These small, local firms or family businesses do not have human resource departments and are not very aware of or interested in concepts like Corporate Social Responsibility. A different and often more personal approach is needed to convince them to review their recruitment policies and consider employing more older people and migrants.

This DP has therefore established contacts with SMEs through a personal visit by one of three counsellors employed in the project. Access to companies has proved relatively easy and employers are willing to share their experiences with older or "non-native" workers. The DP offers a range of support services including better matching, advice on existing employment measures and guidance for the employer and the prospective employee. The counsellors are also available to help candidates with the application process and then continue to provide on-going support and monitoring.

Inan Ureyil, who has a Turkish background, started a placement with EXKI making and selling sandwiches. He

"found it very positive that the Paradox-consultants call me or visit me from time to time in order to see how things are going. In case of problems, I can always go back to them and even if I have no problems, I can always visit their office for a short talk."

Action plan for diversity

The EQUAL project has produced a guide for employers that outlines how to create a Diversity Action Plan. And through direct contacts with SMEs and analysis of jobs adverts, Paradox identified a total of 320 vacancies and 130 placements for members of its target groups. In filling 40% of the vacancies, its placement rates were higher than the public employment service and other employment projects. Over half of these placements have led to more permanent employment.

To promote its success, Paradox has organised events where employers with positive experiences of recruiting people from ethnic minority or older age groups have testified to the benefits of hiring such workers. Similarly, the DP has produced a newsletter designed for and targeted at employers in general. In addition, the project's methodology, results and learning effects have been described in a handbook. A second publication is targeted at counsellors and other professionals who play intermediary or mediation roles in the labour market.

The partnership was developed gradually. The first to join was Randstad – a temporary employment agency with experience of placing older people but mainly in larger companies. Then, as things progressed two other important players came on board: Vitamine W – an NGO that had good contacts with the migrant community – and VDAB – the Flemish Public Employment Service.

From an early stage, it was decided to keep the partnership as small and as manageable as possible but, at the same time, the four partners realised that they would need some external help. Their solution was to establish a group of experts including the city council, employment ministry, local chambers of commerce and a migrant association.

Expertise can help build credibility

This group of experts provided the DP with credibility and contacts, co-financing, advice on the overall direction and a testing ground for its pilot outputs. Through the group, the Antwerp Sub-Regional Employment Committee became aware of the DP's success in helping SMEs draw up Diversity Action Plans and now promotes the DP's approach to other Employment Committees.

> The EQUAL project's innovative form of partnership was one of the keys to its success. It managed to bring together a group of high profile organisations — across the public, private and voluntary sectors — who would otherwise have had few opportunities to work together on this scale.

IDEA Consult, the managing organisation of this EQUAL DP, is convinced that its methodology will be transferred to the wider labour market. The methods and tools will be disseminated throughout Flanders by the Public Employment Service (VDAB) as well as the Sub-Regional Employment Committees and will also be promoted by the Belgian Federation of the Self-Employed. In addition, the results of the project will be transmitted to policy makers in the Flemish and the Federal Employment Ministries. Finally, its outcomes will be presented on the European stage, as Paradox will be featured in a book called "DiverCities" to be published later this year by ENGIME, a Network of Excellence in the EU's Fifth Framework Research Programme.

A more detailed version and other EQUAL success stories can be found at: http://europa.eu.int/comm/employment_social/equal/activities/search_en.cfm

PAR▼DOX

Wie weet wordt diversiteit de kracht van uw onderneming?

Country: Belgium
Region: Flanders
Project name: Paradox – RE-IN+45
Project duration: 30 months
ESF Priority Area: Employability
ESF funding (€): 377 749
Total funding (€): 802 121
National EQUAL partners: Randstad Belgium, VDAB, Vitamine W
Transnational partnership with: Italy, the Netherlands
Contact details:
Anneleen Peeters
IDEA Consult
Congresstraat 37/41 bus 3
B-1000 Brussel
Tel: +32 2 282 17 75
E-mail: anneleen.peeters@ideaconsult.be
Website: www.ideaconsult.be

Constructing Pathways for Personal Progression

Signature of the Good Friday (Belfast) Agreement in Northern Ireland in 1998 brought with it a new sense of optimism within the prison service. It provided the mechanism for release of politically motivated prisoners, so the profile of Northern Ireland's prison population became similar to the rest of Europe. It also marked the beginning of policy changes designed to improve prisoners' employability and resettlement in the community after release.

The Personal Progression System Development Partnership (DP) follows on from two important prison-related policy initiatives. Firstly, a recommendation of the Review of the Criminal Justice System in Northern Ireland of March 2000 stated that "*aftercare and support to discharged prisoners should be adequately resourced.*" Secondly, in 2001, a Joint Thematic Review by the Inspectorates of Prisons and Probation called for "*a national strategy to be drawn up and implemented ... to achieve the effective resettlement of offenders sentenced to imprisonment.*" This DP focused on putting these policies into practice by providing pathways to employment for prisoners and support mechanisms after their release.

Building pathways from inside prison

At the core of the project is the Personal Progression System (PPS). So called PPS workers, employed by the coordinating organisation, the Northern Ireland Association for the Care and Resettlement of Offenders (NIACRO), were placed in three penal institutions: Maghaberry, a high security prison, Magilligan a low to medium security prison, and Hydebank Young Offenders Centre.

The PPS workers carried out employability assessments of individual prisoners and helped to develop resettlement plans to ensure their reintegration after release. They also built up strong working relationships with a range of public sector, private sector, voluntary and community agencies so that different forms of support would be available, sometimes at short notice, as soon as the offenders left the prison gates.

In the Hydebank Young Offenders Centre, the project worked with 40 young men each year, all of whom were at risk of unemployment, re-offending and return to prison. In Maghaberry, the DP targeted annually 60 prisoners with a statutory link to the Probation Board on their release. And at Magilligan, the PPS worker also worked with 60 prisoners per year, focusing in particular on those who intended to stay in the North West area after their release. In the course of the project's lifetime, a total of 429 individuals have benefited from its services and support.

In terms of results, half of the participants maintained contact with the project for the full three months after release. Of these, 25% have found permanent full-time or part-time employment and 40% have gone on to further education or training.

Finalising resettlement plans with the Governor of the Hydebank Young Offenders' Centre

New approaches take hold

The EQUAL project's success can be attributed to several key innovations. Firstly the concept of employability assessments proved particularly valuable. On the basis of each assessment, a prisoner is offered further training to improve their employability, either through the prison's education department or in the community after release. Secondly, the introduction of PPS into the prison has encouraged the different services, such as probation, education and health, to share their assessments and to develop common resettlement plans.

Another important element pioneered by the DP was the detailed planning for the period immediately after release. Every ex-offender has a series of meetings lined up with those agencies that can assist his or her reintegration.

Prisoners get training that match employers' needs

These might include appointments with services such as a housing association, the social security office, the doctor's surgery or a training agency.

The long-term impact of the DP's activities was secured by involving the key agencies responsible for implementing a new strategy. A Strategic Management Group comprising representatives from NIACRO, the Probation Board for Northern Ireland and the Northern Ireland Prison Service took responsibility for the overall direction of the project, while local Steering Groups were established in each of the three prisons. The partnership was clearly successful: the PPS is currently being mainstreamed throughout the Northern Ireland Prison Service.

Employers play their part

Another key area of the DP's work was to encourage employers to provide work experience and job opportunities for ex-offenders. For example, employers and training agencies have been invited into the prisons to meet prisoners and to evaluate their potential either as employees or trainees. Several inmates have carried out work experience with local employers, while still returning each evening to prison. And where appropriate, the DP has introduced new forms of training into the penal institutions such as employers explaining the job requirements of a particular sector or tutors running a business start-up course. Constructive use has also been made of home leave with prisoners starting to contact local agencies and services prior to their release so that their re-integration into their local communities will be as smooth as possible.

This pursuit of change and innovation is reflected in a second round EQUAL project called the ReachOut Programme. The three original partners will be joined by Business in the Community, an employers' organisation in Northern Ireland. This addition will help to ensure a better match between employers' needs and the employability measures proposed through the Personal Progression System.

A more detailed version and other EQUAL success stories can be found at: http://europa.eu.int/comm/employment_social/equal/activities/search_en.cfm

---

Country: United Kingdom
Region: Northern Ireland
Project name: Personal Progression System
Project duration: November 2001 – November 2005
ESF priority area: Employability
ESF funding (€): 897 873
Total funding (€): 1 381 479
National EQUAL partners: Northern Ireland Prison Service (NIPS), Probation Board for Northern Ireland (PBNI), Northern Ireland Association for the Care and Resettlement of Offenders (NIACRO)
Transnational partnership with: Finland, Greece, the Netherlands
Contact details:
NIACRO
Ms Olwen Lyner, Chief Executive Officer
4 Amelia Street
Belfast BT2 7GS
GB-Northern Ireland
Tel: +44 28 9032 0157
E-mail: olwen@niacro.org
Website: www.niacro.co.uk

Telelearning: preparing prisoners for a new life outside

Telfi
Telelernen für HaftinsassInnen

Whilst the number of inmates in Austrian penal institutions has been rising continuously over the past few years, the chances of these offenders being successfully re-integrated into work have been deteriorating steadily. Over half of the 9 000 detainees have had no education or training beyond compulsory schooling. Many of them are affected by an accumulation of other serious problems such as drug addiction, debt, linguistic and cultural difficulties or psychological handicaps. Only one fifth had been in regular employment in the course of the year before their conviction and they are rarely involved in any active labour market measures after their release.

The European Employment Guidelines place a strong emphasis on reinforcing social inclusion and preventing exclusion from the world of work. In a recommendation to Austria on the implementation of employment policies, the EU Council of Ministers stresses the need "...to increase participation in training, especially for the low skilled and for immigrants". The Tele-Learning for Imprisoned People Development Partnership (DP), "Telfi" for short, is a particularly striking example of good practice that addresses this need.

E-learning is a quantum leap for prisons

"The introduction of e-learning in prisons is a quantum leap in the development of training for people in custody" says Walter Hammerschick, who coordinates Telfi's work.

"For a long time, the idea of allowing access to the Internet from jail was perceived as incompatible with the nature of penal institutions. We had to tackle problems that related to the particular conditions of imprisonment, such as security issues, specific legal requirements and also conventional attitudes towards offenders."

Telfi's approach was not driven primarily by the desire to make more effective use of available technology. Its main objective was to integrate these new opportunities into a process of individualised support and empowerment that continues after the prisoner's release. It combines the introduction of flexible, modern training methods, including qualifications relevant to current labour market needs, with a range of accompanying measures to prepare prisoners for their new lives after they walk through the prison gates.

The DP has provided new practical tools and an infrastructure for e-learning in prisons. A central "prison education server" and a server platform have been established that comply with the security requirements of the individual institutions. Readily available learning software has been tested and then adapted to make it suitable for use in prisons.

Preparing for a new life outside

Though participation in the courses is voluntary, the number of people who are interested generally exceeds the number of available places. The course programme, which structures the training and experiences of work during the period of imprisonment to the realities of working and social life outside the institution, is the backbone of the individualised support process piloted by Telfi.

The programme includes a range of courses, enabling participants to progress at a pace that matches their own capabilities. It started with training in literacy and numeracy, language courses and IT basics and was gradually broadened to cover professional fields, such as stock management, metalwork, woodwork and other vocational competences.

Telfi has implemented some 40 telelearning courses that are integrated with individual support plans. These courses were initially aimed at prisoners who were coming close to their release and those who were seen to comply with the rules and requirements of open prison methods. Now they also involve inmates who face longer periods of custody and who, after having successfully completed a course, might take on tutorial functions in future courses.

> "For me, the course has paid off. After my term I will start work in a travel agency. Without evidence of my computing skills I would not have got the job. Also, the computer course is much more demanding than work in the prison's tailoring workshop". Like this prisoner, almost half the detainees, who stayed in contact with Neustart after their release, have found a job on the open labour market or enrolled in a special placement or training programme.

From project partnership to sustainable network

But all this work will not only benefit the 250 participants in the Telfi courses. Since it started, five further prisons have joined the project or indicated a strong interest in cooperating with it. Telfi's new learning platform enables all Austrian prisons to use the software available on the prison education server to organise and deliver e-learning courses. In order to transfer its approach to other prisons, Telfi established a model training course for its tutors which is now part of the regular programme of the Centre for Further and Continuing Education and Training of Staff in the Penal System.

With policy support from strategic partners like the Ministry of Justice, national employment service and social partners, the initial project partnership has developed into a sustainable network with the capacity to promote the DP's approach throughout the Austrian penal system.

Telfi has also been closely involved in Transnational Partnerships with other EQUAL DPs facing similar challenges. They are gradually moving towards a European network to link the experience of seven Member States in the field. Some, including Austria, have selected projects for the second round of EQUAL that will capitalise on the achievements to date.

Transnational solutions for cross-border cases

The PRILEARESNET Transnational Partnership has started developing a European server infrastructure which could benefit a substantial proportion of the Telfi target group. Approximately 4 000 of Austria's inmates do not have Austrian nationality but many are citizens of other EU countries. The use of a common IT platform could provide access to learning opportunities that are recognised in their country of origin. The Dutch partner in this TP has particular experience of working with prisoners who are serving sentences abroad.

For Telfi, the exchange with its transnational partners has had a direct practical effect – as a basis for developing the prison education server and the Illias learning platform. But transnational cooperation has also had significant intangible benefits. The positive lessons learned from innovative experience in other Member States confirmed the validity of Telfi's ambitious, holistic approach. A new Development Partnership called "Step-by-Step" has now been launched to further the experience of Telfi.

A more detailed version and other EQUAL success stories can be found at: http://europa.eu.int/comm/employment_social/equal/activities/ search_en.cfm

Country: Austria
Region: No specific region
Project name: Telelernen für HaftinsassInnen – Telfi
Project duration: September 2002 – September 2005
ESF Priority Area: Employability
ESF funding (€): 498 904
Total funding (€): 997 808
National EQUAL partners: Institut für Rechts- und Kriminalsoziologie and 17 others
Transnational partnership with: Germany, the Netherlands
Contact details:
Institut für Rechts- und Kriminalsoziologie
Walter Hammerschick
Museumstraße 5
A-1016 Wien
Tel: +43 (0) 1 5261516
E-mail: walter.hammerschick@irks.at
Website: www.telfi.at

Innovation

Mainstreaming

Transnationality

Empowerment

Partnership

Managing your own integration

Current trends in Dutch health and welfare policies aim to make the process of reintegrating people with disabilities into work more "demand-driven", giving individuals more responsibility. But for people with disabilities to be able to steer their own reintegration, certain skills and knowledge are necessary to make the process a success.

Empowerment means taking control

The "Vrijbaan" Development Partnership (DP) is trying to replace the more traditional approaches to integration with one that enables people with disabilities to take control of their own integration. It has pioneered a new way to measure the degree of empowerment of disabled people, which can then be used to design the best possible training paths for those furthest from the labour market.

Apart from this tool, the DP has also produced a number of aids to help other bodies develop an empowerment orientation in their work. These include a publication explaining the measuring tool, a handbook to help trainers and coaches develop empowering attitudes, and a manual on empowerment training.

Vrijbaan hopes that other training agencies will be influenced by the initial positive results of its empowerment activities, which have succeeded in increasing the participants' self-confidence and self-image.

Aukje Hendrix from Heerlen had problems walking and also had to overcome the consequences of a minor stroke. She had been an enthusiastic worker in the care sector but now had to find another occupation. After her training she felt that *"I learnt that I am allowed to be the person I am. I'm allowed to make mistakes! This means that I feel much more secure and that has a positive influence on all aspects of life!"*. Peer van Halderen, a 49-year old man with a visual disability, followed the same training course to attempt to get back into a job. He said: *"I thought I had an insight into myself and knew how things worked but the results of some of the training were a real revelation to me."*

Measuring empowerment to strengthen it

When the project started, there was no common concept of empowerment. So the DP created a structured work programme aimed at defining, measuring and strengthening empowerment.

The partnership had been carefully designed to apply the principle of empowerment. In addition to the four Reintegration Centres that originally proposed the project, the DP comprises a local interest group of people with disabilities and the National Disability Council, which advises central government on disability issues. The final partner is the Centre of Expertise on Disability, which is linked to the University of Maastricht and helps to provide credibility for the DP's outcomes.

The Centre of Expertise on Disability led the DP's scientific approach. It developed a concept of empowerment through research and in-depth interviews with clients and practitioners on motivation and assessment of new needs. The next stage was to create an instrument that could measure an individual's level of attainment based on this definition. The questionnaire developed was applied to over 400 people with disabilities who had either found work or were coming towards the end of their reintegration process.

Targeted training helps people into work

The last stage was the establishment of a training system to counteract any empowerment "weaknesses" detected. New training modules were developed and have now been followed by over 100 individuals throughout the country. The final project evaluation showed that the vast majority felt more empowered and that they were now in a better position to enter work and to promote their skills and abilities.

Innovation and staff development seem to be inextricably linked in Vrijbaan and this combination has also permeated into the project's transnational partnership. This cross-border cooperation involved the application of Vrijbaan's techniques to a total of 360 people in three other countries, the joint production of a pack of empowerment resources and two sessions for training trainers in empowerment.

The EQUAL project's experience in strengthening empowerment also spurred it on to a new challenge. They con-

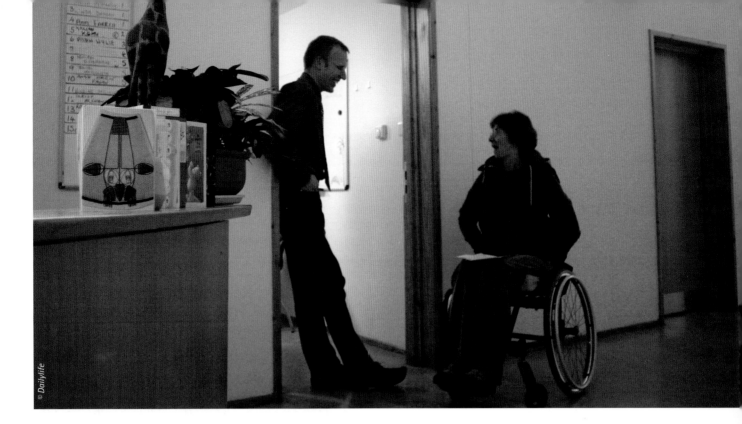

© Dailylife

cluded that empowerment training for people with disabilities alone was not enough – it was also necessary to train personnel in creating an empowering environment to help stimulate and strengthen empowerment amongst their clients. A new EQUAL DP called REQUEST has now been selected to carry out this follow-up work. The fact that this new partnership will involve two major social security bodies is an important testimony to the legacy of innovation that Vrijbaan leaves behind in terms of its clear definition of empowerment, an effective instrument to measure it, and high-quality training to improve it.

A more detailed version and other EQUAL success stories can be found at: http://europa.eu.int/comm/employment_social/equal/activities/ search_en.cfm

Country: the Netherlands (National coverage)
Project name: VrijBaan
Project duration: May 2002 – May 2005
ESF priority area: Employability
ESF funding (€): 782 484 (estimated costs for actions 2 & 3)
Total funding (€): 1 564 968 (estimated costs for actions 2 & 3)
National EQUAL partners: Chronisch Zieken en Gehandicaptenraad, EEGA Educatie, IRV Kenniscentrum voor Revalidatie en Handicap, IvAS-Heliomare, Sonneheerdt Opleiding en Arbeid, Universiteit van Maastricht, Werkenrode, Werkgroep Integratie Gehandicapten
Transnational partnership with: Belgium, Czech Republic, Finland, Austria
Contact details:
Hoensbroeck Centrum voor Arbeidsperspectief
Ms Tessa Zaeyen
Zandbergsweg 111
NL-6432 CC Hoensbroek
Tel: +31 45 528300
E-mail: tzaeyen@werkenrode.nl
Website: www.vrijbaan.nl

Down, but definitely not out

It is all too easy to find yourself left behind in the competitive rat race of modern society. And once you drop out, it can be very hard to climb back in. Factors such as low education levels, unemployment, homelessness, abuse and drug addiction can stack up to form an insuperable barrier to social integration. Self-confidence, once lost, is very hard to rebuild.

> "We want to show policy-makers and the public that marginalised people, in our case people with severe drug problems, are not hopeless cases who need permanent care," says Alec Carlberg of social enterprise Basta Arbetskooperativ. "Given the right surroundings they can produce high quality products and run an efficient company which will amaze ordinary people and fight prejudice."

The Empowerment for the Future Development Partnership has created a good practice model of how an empowerment-based social enterprise can address social problems. It focuses specifically on rehabilitating drug abusers and thereby resolving their problems of unemployment and homelessness.

Colleagues, not clients

The project helps the most vulnerable people, who exist on the fringes of society. They are typically in middle age, and three-quarters are male. They have usually had little education, have been long-term unemployed and are homeless. Many have been victims of physical, emotional or sexual abuse, and many are drug addicts. The main barrier to reintegrating them is their lack of self-confidence.

The DP aimed to find innovative forms of rehabilitation to tackle long-term drug use. The social services pay for one year's rehabilitation, but because Basta is a trading enterprise, people who want to stay can work within the company as long as they feel that they need the security of being a part of a company where no drugs exist, either at work or after hours. People are not considered as "clients"; during the first year they are apprentices and after that, if they choose to stay on, they become colleagues. This is of great psychological importance in the rehabilitation process.

Basta offers its members job training and coaching to set up a new business. The qualification they get after one year's study both strengthens their self-esteem and prepares them for real working life – both vocationally and psychologically.

Re-awakening an old tradition

Empowerment by self-organisation among poor and marginalised people was downplayed in recent years as a method of tackling severe social problems in Sweden. But this project has re-awoken an old tradition of self-organisation through social enterprise. This revival has benefits for both marginalised people and society as a whole. Individuals gain a stable and secure livelihood, while society enjoys an economically efficient way of tackling problems in the modern welfare state.

Empowerment for the Future's example has now inspired a second group in Gothenburg to set up a similar enterprise. It is now recognised by social services departments, who recommend it to drug users wanting to reform.

The project has a competitive edge when bidding for municipal contracts to offer therapy services to drug users because it only needs to earn around half its income

Qualifications strengthen self-esteem

Graffiti removal is one service offered by the social enterprise

from its therapy work. The other half comes from the sale of goods and services such as construction, graffiti removal, design, carpentry, a dog kennel and vocational training. This productive activity is an integral part of the alternative rehabilitation process and brings in around half the co-operative's income.

A return on society's investment

A cost-benefit analysis of the value added for society of enterprises like Basta is now being carried out. Preliminary studies show that even if a drug user stays at Basta for one year, and then goes back to his old life, society reaps a 50% return on its investment in terms of reduced cost of healthcare and crime. If that person succeeds in holding down a job and stays on at Basta, then social profitability rises as he starts to pay into the benefit system rather than being a drain on it.

The different skills and experiences of the DP's partner organisations fitted together well. Basta provided the experience of setting up a co-operative integration enterprise, and FUNK the contacts on the ground in the Gothenburg area. The University of Lund contributed evaluation expertise, and once it has assessed the project's results, insurer Folksam is a possible vector to multiply the experience more broadly.

Empowerment for the Future is also active at European level. With its partners abroad, it has created a one-year university course aimed at adults marginalised by their lack of a basic school education. The course teaches people how to manage social enterprises in a more efficient and businesslike way, and combines distance learning with modules taught at universities in Lund, London, Paris and Murcia. Twenty students have qualified so far.

The DP and its partners have also created an international social enterprise called ECCO (European Community Co-operative Observatory). One service under development in the next round of EQUAL is consultancy in the new EU member states on starting up new social enterprises. And in addition to partners from Britain, France, Spain and Italy, Hungary is now joining the team.

A more detailed version and other EQUAL success stories can be found at: http://europa.eu.int/comm/employment_social/equal/activities/search_en.cfm

Country: Sweden
Region: National coverage, but main activities in the Municipality of Nykvarn and around Gothenburg
Project name: Egenmakt för Framtiden (Empowerment For the Future)
Project duration: January 2002 – June 2005
ESF priority area: Entrepreneurship
ESF funding (€): 698 961
Total funding (€): 1 463 252
National EQUAL partners: Basta Arbetskooperativ, FUNK (Funktionell Narkoman), School of Social Work at the University of Lund, Folksam
Transnational partnership with: UK, France, Spain, Italy
Contact details:
Basta arbetskooperativ
Alec Carlberg
S-155 92 NYKVARN
Tel: +46 8 552 41400
E-mail: alec.carlberg@basta.se
Website: www.basta.se

Innovation

Mainstreaming

Transnationality ▶

Empowerment

Partnership ▶

Breaking with tradition

In Germany there is no shortage of support for people who want to set up in business. In fact, in 2003 alone 430 000 previously unemployed people started their own business. But all too often business support centres are failing to attract potential entrepreneurs from disadvantaged groups, including women, young people, ethnic minorities, and people with disabilities.

The EXZEPT Development Partnership (DP) was set up to fill this gap – offering better access to both loans and business advice. Its aim is to ensure that support providers, like regional public authorities, financial institutions, both accept and provide for the specific needs of these target groups.

Responding to real needs

As a first step, the EXZEPT DP carried out a thorough investigation into the specific problems of the target groups, and the tools needed to help them go into business. Similar studies have been carried out by DPs in other countries, which are cooperating with EXZEPT under the transnational partnership known as CEFT. Together these studies provide invaluable (and in some cases the only existing) empirical material on which to design policies that respond to real rather than supposed needs.

For example, realising that few women use start-up centres, EXZEPT tried to identify their specific needs when setting up in business. Based on this research, EXZEPT developed a guide with 27 key criteria for taking account of gender in support services. One of its recommendations is that a specific team member takes overall responsibility for gender issues. It also highlights the need for access to adequate childcare and public transport, and to screen information and training provision to ensure men and women are treated equally.

Staff from business support centres in Cologne, Mainz, Hamburg and Potsdam, specialised in dealing with migrant workers, helped to determine the criteria for success of start-ups among migrant communities. EXZEPT partners found that migrants often need more individual coaching because of their diverse backgrounds. Business plans also need to take account of family involvement in the business.

Dagmar Rissler, a coach at Enigma in Hamburg and one of the EXZEPT partners, comments: "*migrants often take the support of family or friends for granted, without actually asking the people concerned. This can lead to unrealistic financial and personnel assumptions. They also often have overoptimistic expectations about earnings. A coach can help to verify assumptions and to estimate income more realistically.*"

An entry point to all support services

Before designing new tools and methods to reach out to disadvantaged groups, EXZEPT conducted a detailed survey of existing start-up support. The result was to design a regional one-stop-shop (OSS) model. The idea is not that the one-stop-shops provide the complete range of support services, but rather that they guide clients to the existing and new service providers in a given region, according to the type of business and stage of development.

To work effectively, one-stop-shops must therefore be well connected with existing regional networks and cooperate with traditional institutions such as the employment agency, local banks, the local authority and the chamber of commerce. The success of the EXZEPT DP is largely due to the fact its partners cover different stages and aspects of business support.

For example, GLS Gemeinschaftsbank, the oldest and largest ethical and ecological bank in Germany, was a key partner. They helped develop the microcredit model which draws upon the experience of other initiatives in Germany, plus that of other DPs working in the CEFT transnational partnership. It involves a four-point system for obtaining a loan – personality check, concept check, market check and risk check – to decide whether guarantees or peer lending are used. This is followed up by a clearly defined system of aftercare, comprising individual coaching, group coaching and self-evaluation.

Back to business for many

The EXZEPT one-stop-shop model has been successfully put into practice in Offenbach, Tauberbischofsheim and Darmstadt. These three agencies supported about 2 500 people in 2003-2004, and helped an impressive number of them to reclaim their working lives. Sylvie Feindt, a consultant for EXZEPT, says: "*the figures on one OSS show that 85% of the people it supported either started their own company or entered employment.*"

A big boost for microfinance

The activities of the EXZEPT DP are already influencing business start-up support initiatives throughout Germany. A newsletter ("Gründung Aktuell") set up by the DP to present the work and different perspectives of those engaged in start-up support continues to be published, although the DP has formally ended (www.gruendung-aktuell.de).

But it is the field of microfinance where the experience of the EXZEPT DP is having strongest impact. EXZEPT and other microfinance initiatives have developed a common model for microcredit under the current German Credit Services Act. In April 2004 they set up the German Mikrofinanz Institut (MFI). This now consists of more than 50 organisations from all German regions. At its initial general meeting, MFI was supported by the federal government bank that supports SMEs – Kreditanstalt für Wiederaufbau (KfW), the Federal Ministry for Economics and Labour and the Federal Employment Services.

> "*Micro start-ups need particular support. If we want a strong self-employed sector, we have to put innovative ideas into practice. The first hurdle is often small business credit. Microfinance institutions elsewhere are providing effective support at this particular point. It is time that this successful model was also taken up in Germany.*" Christine Scheel, chairwoman of the finance committee of the German Bundestag.

A more detailed version and other EQUAL success stories can be found at: http://europa.eu.int/comm/employment_social/equal/activities/search_en.cfm

One beneficiary now provides services in wound treatment and chiropody

Country: Germany
Regions: Hessen (HE); Nordrhein Westfalen (NW); Hamburg (HH)
Project name: EXZEPT – Erleichterung von Existenzgründungen durch Akzeptanz
Project duration: January 2002 – April 2005
ESF priority area: Entrepreneurship
ESF funding (€): 2 244 479
Total funding (€): 4 746 094
National EQUAL partners: Exzept GmbH Offenbach, KIZ GmbH Offenbach, GLS Gemeinschaftsbank Bochum, Deutsches Mikrofinanz Institut e.V. Berlin, Enigma Gründerwerft Hamburg, SFC Köln, Gründernetzwerk e.V.
Strategic partners: Dr Schulze-Böing, Stadt Offenbach, Agentur für Arbeit (Hamburg, Offenbach, Hessisches Wirtschaftsministerium
Transnational partnership with: UK, the Netherlands, Czech Republic
Contact details:
Exzept GmbH
Dr Bernd Curtius
Odenwaldring 38
D-69063 Offenbach
Tel: +49 69 84 84 78 150
E-mail: berndcurtius@exzept.de
Website: www.exzept.de, www.mikrofinanz.net

A regional partnership for inclusive entrepreneurship

The Spanish Basque country has experienced severe industrial restructuring over the past few decades. However, thanks to a long tradition of public-private partnerships and an advanced social economy, new economic activities have sprung up to offset the costs of factory closures.

Part of this success can be attributed to the creation of a network of 23 local development agencies, called Garapen, which covers all three provinces of the Basque Country and three-quarters of the population. This is the only regional network for encouraging business creation of its kind in Spain, and is one of the most complete in Europe.

Garapen is the lead partner of an EQUAL project called Red Accent (Accent Network). The objectives were twofold: firstly, to enable network members to share lessons and develop common approaches to support business creation; and secondly, to work with other regional actors to strengthen business support such as creating an entrepreneurial culture in schools, improving access to finance and increasing the sustainability of start-ups.

Learning from one another

The local development agencies that make up the Garapen network combine services normally associated with employment offices, with activities focusing on the creation and modernisation of small businesses. It enables each agency to have a more global view of problems in the local labour market and to develop integrated solutions. But, up to now, the pressure of day-to-day business has prevented them from learning from each other. EQUAL has allowed a clear transfer of information and know-how from one organisation to another.

Through a series of joint meetings Accent developed an inventory of 18 different support methodologies. These have been organised into a menu for each of four different stages of setting up and consolidating a firm, and placed onto a common intranet accessible to all members.

The next step was to train a group of trainers to transfer the successful methods from one agency to another. For example an employee from the Bilbao agency, Lan Ekintza, has trained the other 22 agencies in a successful programme they use to encourage the unemployed to identify and implement their own business ideas.

Some of the agencies then carried out pilot projects to test the methods in their own local area. Almost 700 potential entrepreneurs were involved in these tests, most of whom were women. Most pilots focused on the early stages of creating a business culture and the later stages of consolidating start-ups.

On-line services improve access

Another result of the network collaboration was a joint internet portal that provides on-line business support and advice for entrepreneurs. It includes a training programme on entrepreneurship skills, that has attracted over 100 participants, 65 of whom have since set up in business. The on-line business advice service has been very successful. During the first eight months of operation, 290 people received advice, 47% of whom were women.

Cradle to grave business support

The sharing of support methodologies highlighted the fact that the agencies were generally strong in start-up advice and helping to develop the business plan, but far weaker in the earlier stages of creating an entrepreneurial culture in schools and training centres, and in the later stages of building bridges with the world of finance and post start-up advice.

By collaborating with different partners, the local development agencies were able to develop tools and services that fill the gaps in business support. For example, working with schools across the province, they tested several imaginative tools designed to introduce students and teachers to the world of entrepreneurship. One such tool is a Monopoly-style board game called Imagine your own company which takes young teenagers through the key decisions involved in each stage of setting up a company.

> *"Keeping someone in unemployment benefit for a year costs the state about € 43 000, but supporting a job in the social economy costs only half that."*
> Sepp Eisenriegler, Manager of the Vienna repair network RUSZ

tion. It offers services that are not yet available on the market, gives support and mentoring to its employees and raises public awareness of ecological and labour market issues – Graz is an EU "Eco-city" and Ökoservice was selected as a Local Agenda 21 good practice. It has opened a branch in St Veit am Vogau, 40 km south of Graz, and an extension to Vienna is under consideration.

Traditional crafts are also involved

In addition to social enterprises, many traditional crafts are built on the idea of durability and repair, and so jewellers, watchmakers, cobblers, tailors, plumbers, carpenters, electricians and bicycle shops have all joined the networks. RepaNet members agree a quality standard which commits them to attempt any reasonable repair, to deal with at least five different brands of equipment, and to charge a set amount for a binding quotation.

The project has a vision that builds from the bottom up to European level. Thanks to the support of EQUAL, the RepaNet model has spread from Vienna and Graz to five other regions in Austria. Altogether, the five enterprises employ 90 people and repair 4 000 items of equipment a year. Each repair centre has its own speciality: in Graz it's audio, video and computers, in Liezen white goods, in Ried-im-Innkreis bicycles, in Vienna computers – and multifunctional Hohenems tackles white goods, computers and bicycles. Under the aegis of the national federation, two more regional networks are in their formative stages.

Swapping good ideas across Europe

The national federation Reparaturnetzwerk Österreich is in turn a member of the European network RREUSE (Recycling and Reuse European Social Enterprises), which was established four years ago. As well as lobbying for policy change, this network helps its members to develop the best delivery mechanisms. Its 1 000 member enterprises employ 16 000 people across ten countries of Europe. In March 2004, RREUSE members came to Graz to take part in the exchange mart the RepaNet DP organised within their transnational

partnership SENECA. It allowed them to swap ideas for new environmental businesses in the social economy.

RepaNet's work is being taken forward in two new development partnerships in the second round of EQUAL: Econet Austria will focus on setting up integration firms in the recycling of electronic waste, while Public Social Private Partnership aims to take social enterprise into new fields.

A more detailed version and other EQUAL success stories can be found at: http://europa.eu.int/comm/employment_social/equal/activities/ search_en.cfm

Country: Austria
Region: No specific region
Project name: RepaNet – Reparaturnetzwerk Österreich
Project duration: September 2002 – September 2005
ESF priority area: Entrepreneurship
ESF funding (€): 1 016 292
Total funding (€): 2 032 584
National EQUAL partners: Arbeitsgemeinschaft Müllvermeidung and 12 national partners
Transnational partnership with: Czech Republic, Finland, Italy
Contact details:
ARGE Müllvermeidung
Berthold Schleich
Dreihackengasse 1
AT-8020 Graz
Tel: +43 316 71 23 09
E-mail: schleich@arge.at
Website: www.repanet.at

The right type of money

Sant Cosme in Barcelona faces challenges familiar to many old industrial neighbourhoods across Europe. Restructuring has dramatically cut the number of job opportunities for local people and unemployment stands at around 25%. Migrants make up nearly two-thirds of the population. Many local residents are forced to survive through a combination of social security payments and the informal economy.

The EQUAL project "Sant Cosme Innova" was set up to test a particular blend of microfinance and business support as a route out of social exclusion. A survey of local people without stable employment revealed that 80% of them were interested in self-employment, but that getting access to a loan to start a business was virtually impossible. Most people not only lacked the necessary collateral, but also the confidence and experience to put their case to the bank.

Understanding and supporting clients through partnership

The project partnership brought together a large financial institution – in this case Fundació Un Sol Món, part of the Caixa de Catalunya – with the local social services and other frontline support workers. A non-governmental organisation specialised in providing employment advice to disadvantaged people (Fundación FIAS) offered mentoring services, helping clients along the path to self-employment. This division of work between the partners of the project provided a model for microfinance initiatives.

The basic product offered by Un Sol Món was a small, flexible loan from as little as €600 to a maximum of €15 000 (the average was €8 000) with a fixed 6% interest rate. The specific terms of the loan were tailored each person's needs by using "step-lending" methods. Initially, loans were made in small amounts and for short periods, but could be increased in a series of progressive "steps".

No collateral was required. The only guarantee was the solidity of the business plan prepared in conjunction with Pla d'Actuació de Sant Cosme, the EQUAL partner specialised in providing business support and guidance to disadvantaged groups. They developed a simplified form to collect and evaluate all the relevant financial information about the business idea. Un Sol Món also developed a new programme of financial capacity building for their

clients, to help them stick to the "steps" associated with the loans and to use the finance as an investment rather than just a one-off hand out.

Long-term commercial viability is crucial

The microcredit fund set up by Un Sol Món has now made around 600 loans with a total value of €6 million. An estimated 1 000 jobs have been created, predominantly benefiting women and ethnic minorities. And according to an impact evaluation among the clients, 80% of borrowers have become more prosperous and 70% consider that the microcredit has stabilised their business.

This is the case of Maribel who had worked as a hairdresser for eight years, mostly in the informal economy. Two years ago she obtained a microcredit from Un Sol Món to open her own salon. "*I am very happy with the business. I have hired two workers and I am planning to open a new hairdresser's in El Prat de Llobregat,*" she says.

Ninety per cent of the initiatives supported by the microcredit fund are still in business after one year, and defaults are within normal commercial limits. Default rates for the whole fund are around 6%, and management costs are under the rigorous Structural Funds ceiling of 5%. Even if a small proportion of the loans are not repaid, the vast majority of public and private investment returns to the fund and becomes available for further rounds of lending.

EQUAL's role in the project was to contribute €150 000 of capital, which was matched by Un Sol Món to create an earmarked fund of €300 000 for direct financial support to business in this particularly deprived neighbourhood of Barcelona. The loans provided through EQUAL are directed at people in Sant Cosme, who are far further from the labour market than most clients.

New businesses need simplified procedures

The EQUAL project clearly helped to improve access to finance and support. But still many businesses are unable to take the leap into the formal economy. The local authority of Sant Cosme and Fundació Un Sol Món have

Microcredit from Un Sol Mol helped this new business start-ups in Sant Cosme

therefore recommended simpler administrative procedures for becoming self-employed, and mechanisms to allow people to pay the cost of setting up a business in stages. They argue that finance and business services also need to be backed with more progressive tax regimes that smooth the transition from the informal to the formal economy. Unemployment benefit should be extended to cover the early stages of starting a business, and changes in the legal situation of migrant worker are also called for.

These experiences reflect the statements presented in the EU's integrated guidelines for growth and jobs, whose guideline 10 urges improved access to finance for start-ups and existing SMEs.

> *"More than four-fifths of the clients of the EQUAL fund have an income of less than €15 000 a year, a much higher proportion than our clients in general,"* says Isabel Paganobarraga, the fund manager. *"EQUAL allowed us to test out more flexible methods suitable for extremely deprived neighbourhoods, groups such ethnic minorities and people in the informal economy. Since then we have applied many of these methods across the rest of the fund."*

A more detailed version and other EQUAL success stories can be found at: http://europa.eu.int/comm/employment_social/equal/activities/ search_en.cfm

Country: Spain
Region: Cataluña
Project name: Sant Cosme Innova
Project duration: May 2002 – December 2004
ESF priority area: Entrepreneurship
ESF funding (€): 770 518
Total funding (€): 1 541 036
National EQUAL partners: Ayuntamiento El Prat de Llobregat, Fundación Un Sol Món, Fundación FIAS, ADIGSA, Generalitat de Cataluña, UGT del Baix Llobregat, Union Comarcal Baix Llobregat del Sindicato CONC
Transnational partnership with: France
Contact details:
Ayuntamiento El Prat De Llobregat
Xavier Garriga
Plaça de la Vila, s/n
E-8820 El Prat del Llobregat
Tel: +34 93 3790050
E-mail: martinp@aj-elprat.es
Website: www.unsolmon.org

Migrating out of the informal economy

About 30 million people work in the informal economy in Western Europe, far more than the number of unemployed. And over the last decade, the number has increased in nearly all EU countries. To tackle this problem, the EU has urged governments to create a more entrepreneurial culture, to integrate minorities and to review tax and benefit systems so as to make work pay.

The covert nature of the issue means that there is very little information about the people who work in the informal economy, but the EQUAL project Supporting Income Generating Activities among Ethnic Groups and Communities set out to fill the gap. It was led by ADIE (Association pour le Droit à l'Initiative Economique), the largest dedicated microcredit operator in western Europe, with the French national employment agency (Agence Nationale pour l'Emploi – ANPE) and three other organisations as partners.

The Development Partnership (DP) started in 2002 with pilot research and test activities in four deprived urban neighbourhoods in the Paris area. It deliberately chose a target group that could not be further from the stereotype of an entrepreneur: 86% were migrants from sub-Saharan Africa, 76% were women and 35% were illiterate.

Dispelling myths

The pilot research immediately allowed the DP to dispel certain common myths about those who work in the informal economy. For example, contrary to expectations, most people involved have an extremely strong work ethic.

Making ends meet – microcredit helped draper Mrs Rochefort set up in business

Similarly, for most it is not a question of evading the law but of surviving. 40% of the project's beneficiaries were in employment, but earned very low wages. Project workers also found that there was no need to encourage people to start up new activities and businesses: they were already busy doing it.

With this information, the project designed and rolled out an innovative credit and support mechanism to cover the whole Paris area. The aim was to help its clients to build up their income step by step – hopefully to the point where they found it was worth their while to leave the informal economy.

The project achieved three things. First, it provided insights into the social reality of groups that employment policy usually ignores. Secondly, it made several innovations in microlending and business support methodology. Finally, the project used its experience to press for legislative changes.

Peer lending reduces default rates

The DP introduced three successful innovations that stemmed directly from the initial pilot activity. The first was to use word of mouth channels within ethnic networks to reach out into minority communities. The second was to develop a tailor-made blend of step and peer lending techniques. ADIE rejects the idea of simply subsidising or grant-aiding excluded groups, and lends at a commercial rate of interest (of around 6% in 2004). The loans usually start very small, at around €1 000, but once they are repaid they can increase in small steps up to €5 000. They are made to peer groups of three people who take joint responsibility for the loan, thus over-coming the problem of lack of collateral. This technique reduces the default rate too, as one client testifies: "*Without the group I would be afraid to take out a loan. But it's shameful if one cannot make a repayment. It's a question of honour.*" The method also allows loan officers to deal with three parallel applications at a time.

In the third innovation, the project designed a support package of introductory finance courses covering household budget management, the risks of consumer loans, calculating income and expenditure and stock and cash-flow management. Additional modules were designed to help the clients to plan their business and assess the risks and benefits of becoming self-employed or registering a business.

Easing the transition to formal work

In December 2004, after just over two years of operation, the project had created 100 peer-lending groups and provided loans to 275 people. On average, default rates for the clients of the EQUAL project were only 2.6% compared to 5.9% for all of ADIE's clients. So the approach appears to be sustainable, even for these very hard to reach groups. ADIE also has a detailed monitoring system for all its clients, which allows it to plot what works and what doesn't work.

The mainstream solutions promoted by the DP have taken two directions. The first has been to extend the successful microcredit and support techniques piloted by ADIE both in France and the rest of Europe. ADIE now has over 100 branches throughout France, with 300 employees and 700 volunteers and also chairs the European Microcredit Network. The DP's results have been taken up in Spain, Germany and other countries.

The second mainstreaming strategy has been to lobby for legislative changes to ease the transition from the informal to the formal economy. The strategy has met with success: several of the DP's findings have already been incorporated into the French law on social cohesion, and other changes are being campaigned for at a national level.

Alain Mundinger of the Agence Nationale pour l'Emploi says: "*The project has allowed us to gain a real insight into the lives of marginalised groups, and to understand why they choose the informal economy. We plan to spread this information through our agency and study how to further adapt various laws.*"

A more detailed version and other EQUAL success stories can be found at: http://europa.eu.int/comm/employment_social/equal/activities/ search_en.cfm

"There's no need to encourage people to set up a business. They're already doing it."

Country: France
Region: Ile de France
Project name: Appui aux activités génératrices de revenu dans les réseaux ethniques ou communautés (Supporting income generating activities among ethnic groups and communities)
Project duration: May 2002 – December 2004
ESF priority area: Entrepreneurship
ESF funding (€): 297 313
Total funding (€): 569 092
National EQUAL partners: Agence Nationale pour l'Emploi (ANPE), Fédération des Associations Franco-Africaines de Développement (FAFRAD), Institut de Recherche et de Formation Education Cultures Développement (IRFED Europe), Maison de l'Initiative Economique Locale (MIEL)
Transnational partnership with: Spain
Contact details:
Association pour le Droit à l'Initiative Economique (ADIE)
Estelle Mille
4 boulevard Poissonnière
F-75009 Paris
Tel: +33 1 56 03 59 00
E-mail: e.mille@adie.org
Website: www.adie.org

Innovation

Mainstreaming

Transnationality

Empowerment

Partnership

Passport to enterprise

Since reunification, unemployment in Germany has remained stubbornly high. In the country as a whole, almost five million people are out of work, while in the Eastern Länder the unemployment rate hovers around 20%. Young people are among the worst affected.

But one of the more promising developments in recent years has been the increasing number of unemployed people that set up in business. In 2004, the jobless accounted for 360 000 business start-ups, compared to some 100 000 in 1999. For young people with motivation, commitment and ideas, setting up in business often offers a promising route out of unemployment.

Getting young people on board

The objective of the EQUAL Development Partnership (DP), Verbund Enterprise, was to design and promote a model of business support targeted specifically at the young unemployed. It builds on the experience of a pilot project set up in 1999 in the Länder of Brandenburg and Berlin and the experience of the Prince's Trust, which over 25 years has helped almost 60 000 young people set up in business in the UK.

According to the project partners, the Verbund support *"starts where traditional institutions usually stop: it supports young unemployed people with minimal opportunities who seek personal and material independence through a specially designed pathway or ladder into self-employment."*

New models of enterprise support

Verbund Enterprise's main achievement has been to develop a distinctive support methodology. At the heart of its approach is a structured business support pathway made up of four clearly defined stages: profiling (lasting about four weeks); planning (3-12 months); start-up (approximately six months), and consolidation and growth (3-5 years). Each stage involves the several optional services (counselling, training and qualification, mentoring and access to microcredit) to help the entrepreneur acquire the personal competences, skills and resources necessary for success.

Another contribution has been to change the concept of a "one-stop-shop". It no longer tries to do everything under one roof, but rather aims to coordinate inputs from grassroots youth organisations, mainstream business advisers and financial institutions into a tailor-made package of support for young people. During each phase of the support pathway, the DP pulls in different specialist and mainstream providers to provide specific services.

The model includes individual counselling and access to start-up capital, including a specially designed microcredit fund (for example a loan of up to €5 000 for four years at a 5% rate of interest with no security required). It has been found that the microcredits both attract young people and help to build a longer-term relationship with financial institutions.

But one of the problems encountered with a multi-stakeholder system like this was how to ensure quality along the entire pathway. Verbund Enterprise therefore designed an Enterprise Quality Management Structure (EQS), which covers all four stages of the support system.

Sustainable jobs – for less

The results of the Enterprise network are impressive. Over 3 000 young people have used the service, 500 businesses have been started, and more than 750 jobs have been created since 2002. Some 85% of these jobs have gone to young unemployed people, and 45% to women. Survival rates after three years are over 70%.

Moreover, the support required to help young people create a job costs much less than the traditional subsidies provided to attract industry. The EQUAL partnership calculates that the cost of its system is €6 000 per job in an inner city location and €8 000 in a rural area. Given unemployment benefits of around €750 a month this means that, in the city, the costs are recouped after eight months' self-employment.

Another result of the DP's work has been to create an "enterprise passport" which provides a clear and transparent road map of the progress made by the entrepreneur. The Berlin Volksbank has accepted the enterprise passport as a key tool to evaluate the performance of young business starters, and fast-tracks passport holders when they apply for a microloan. Several other business support institutions are interested in using the passport and the Berlin and German governments are considering whether to develop a complementary coaching passport.

Just one of the small businesses helped by EQUAL

> "I have been to a few other institutions providing business start-up support before, but most of them were simply too bureaucratic and donnish," says Claudia Otto, a nutritionist at Aerobic and Fitness in the town of Oranienburg, just north of Berlin. "At Enterprise this was completely different. The project is perfectly suited to young people."

Setting the standard for the future

The Enterprise network has now been extended to other parts of Germany. There are now ten offices, 16 advisers and a pool of more than 100 mentors operating in Berlin, Brandenburg, Lower Saxony, Saxony and Mecklenberg-Vorpommern. One of the partners, iQ Gesellschaft für innovative Qualifizierung e.V., has been responsible for training and transferring successful methods to other parts of the country.

The National Association of German Start-up Initiatives (VDG) is another key outcome of this and other DPs in Germany. It now counts more than 40 members and, among other things, has developed a ten-point charter on improving support for business start-ups by unemployed people.

Verbund Enterprise has also been centrally involved in the creation of the German Microfinanz Institut, which now brings together more than 50 organisations concerned with the financial side of start-ups. Based on the experience of its members, the MFI is developing and spreading innovative forms of microlending in Germany.

A more detailed version and other EQUAL success stories can be found at: http://europa.eu.int/comm/employment_social/equal/activities/ search_en.cfm

Country: Germany
Region: Berlin, Brandenburg
Project name: Verbund Enterprise – Junge Menschen auf dem Weg in die Selbständigkeit
Project duration: January 2002 – June 2005
ESF priority area: Entrepreneurship
ESF funding (€): 3 202 634
Total funding (€): 5 124 117
National EQUAL partners: 11 partners including social enterprises, private companies and non-governmental organisations.
Transnational partnership with: UK, France, Greece, Belgium
Contact details:
JugendLOK e.V. Berlin
Frau Maria Kiczka-Halit
Seumestraße 7/8
D-10245 Berlin
Tel: +49 030 29779733
E-mail: kiczka-halit@jugendlok.de; mashofer@jugendlok.de
Website: www.enterprise-netz.de

Innovation ▶

Mainstreaming

Transnationality

Empowerment

Partnership ▶

Never too old to build a future

In France, people tend to stop working much earlier than the official legal retirement age of 65, on average as early as 57.5. This causes severe problems in some sectors, where the number of people entering the workforce is substantially lower than the number leaving. One example is the building industry, with 1 out of 5 employees over 50 and a need to recruit 65 000 people a year to replace those leaving the sector. As a result, companies are looking at ways to encourage those over 50 to stay in work until the normal retirement age.

The Ages et Travail dans le BTP (Ages and work in the public construction sector) Development Partnership (DP) responded to this need by bringing together a group of organisations to try and reverse this trend. The DP is led by the National Association for Adult Professional Training (AFPA) and involves the French Building Federation (FFB).

Early retirement puts experience at risk

It decided to focus on further strengthening the skills and abilities of older workers, while developing new work opportunities to take account of their wealth of experience. To avoid losing these valuable experiences through early retirement, the DP also recognised the need to promote intergenerational solidarity and learning – so that young people learn to value the experience of their older colleagues.

How can older workers feel more appreciated and, more importantly, how can they be encouraged to keep working? To answer this question, it was important to gain a better understanding of how companies deal with older workers. For the first time in France, the DP conducted a nation-wide survey to map the people and career management structures and processes of nearly 2 700 companies in the building sector. The survey was followed up with more than 60 in-depth case studies.

This exercise provided evidence of what most already expected. Both at political and company level, there is a tendency to concentrate more on the development of young people, which has restricted the learning and career opportunities for older generations. On the other hand, the interest of older workers in further training was also substantially lower, and their age caused several physical and cultural problems that decreased their productivity. On the positive side, however, the survey highlighted the much higher skills levels of senior employees, and increased workplace safety that resulted.

Valuing skills, identifying gaps

Ages et Travail used both the positive and negative findings to develop experimental approaches to better manage the skills of older workers and ensure that their expertise can be effectively transferred to their younger colleagues. These included services to assist managers in mapping the skills base of their current employees and finding more efficient ways of hiring new staff while matching skills gaps and needs. Companies were often surprised by the high level of skills they already had in-house and felt encouraged to offer better positions to senior employees. Older workers were also successfully involved in the recruitment process and provided advice on what was important to look for in a new staff member.

The DP also developed "collective team" working methods and workshop techniques, which put experienced workers and new recruits together and helped them to jointly identify the most important skills required by the job and the best ways to transfer and share these. Finally, Ages et Travail advised companies on how some simple adjustments to the working environment could greatly improve the comfort of the work place for older workers.

> "I worked out solutions with a consultant for each ageing worker. I named a "super tutor" to manage teams made up of seniors and young people. I wanted the staff's knowledge to remain inside the company so I encouraged the senior tutors by giving them a special status. Everybody is satisfied. It is a long term strategy for attracting and retaining newcomers and older workers". Christian Soubre, head of a construction company with 20 workers (including four over 45, and four over 50 years of age).

One construction company appointed employees as tutors to pass on their knowledge

Encouraging dialogue and shared learning

The new approaches tested by the DP have given a new impetus to a sector that until recently was considered as traditional and conservative. The innovative methods helped to introduce new principles of human resource management, such as maximising the use of existing skills and abilities, team working and recognition of prior learning. By promoting dynamic ways to manage and recruit people, and by encouraging dialogue and a sharing of learning between generations, Ages et Travail not only boosted the mobility and empowerment of older workers, but also strongly improved their image.

"Through EQUAL, we have created much better working conditions and helped companies to successfully put these into practice. Ages et Travail created a model which can be easily transferred to other regions and sectors," said Thierry Rosenzweig, the AFPA European project manager.

A more detailed version and other EQUAL success stories can be found at: http://europa.eu.int/comm/employment_social/equal/activities/search_en.cfm

Country: France
Region: Six regions – Limousin, Midi-Pyrénées, Rhône-Alpes, Poitou-Charente, Ile de France
Project name: Ages et Travail dans le BTP
Project duration: May 2002 – February 2005
ESF priority area: Adaptability
ESF funding (€): 640 000
Total funding (€): 1 313 867
National EQUAL partners: Association des Fédérations Régionales et départementales du Bâtiment de Poitou, Centre d'Etudes de Recherches et de Formation du BTP, Fédération Française du Bâtiment, Groupement d'Action Sociale du BTP du Nord-Est, Institut Technique de la FFB, REBATIR, SUP'REHA Formation Conseil
Transnational partnership with: Germany, UK
Contact details:
AFPA (Association Nationale pour la Formation Professionnelle des Adultes)
Thierry Rosenzweig
13 Place du Général de Gaulle
F-93108 Montreuil Cedex
Tel: +33 1 48 70 50 25
E-mail: thierry.rosenzweig@afpa.fr
Website: www.afpa.fr

Innovation

Mainstreaming

Transnationality

Empowerment

Partnership

Investing in local communities for a better future

London's thriving economy is leading to large-scale development across the City. The buoyancy of the construction economy is placing pressures on the industry's employers, 98% of whom face difficulties in recruiting skilled staff to fill vacancies. But many of these areas of regeneration and development are side-by-side areas of deprivation and high unemployment. Many residents, particularly those from ethnic minority and other disadvantaged groups, experience difficulties in finding and sustaining employment.

The Building London – Creating Futures Development Partnership (DP), led by the London Borough of Southwark, was set up to bridge this gap. It aimed to reach out to groups traditionally under represented in the industry, such as women and black and ethnic minority communities, whilst at the same time ensuring that job seekers are suitably qualified and experienced to meet the skills needs of the employers. As Councillor Nick Stanton, Leader of Southwark Council, and lead DP partner said, "*Southwark is a London borough of extremes. In parts, unemployment is four times the national average, yet in others developers have struggled to deliver major construction projects because of severe skills shortages. Building London Creating Futures is bridging this gap*".

Support to women and other underrepresented groups was an important aim of Building London

Partnership with a local focus

Building London Creating Futures is a partnership of construction employers, local authorities, regeneration partnerships, training providers and community organisations. Together, partners have developed a sustainable model of cooperation and coordination to ensure that capital investment in an area benefits local people. After a small-scale pilot funded through the London Development Agency, the partnership's innovative model of "intermediary support" has been rolled out across London under EQUAL.

> "*Building London Creating Futures is a unique employment partnership for the construction industry. Investing in local communities in this way is crucial if the construction industry is to resolve its skills issues.*"
> Bob White, Chairman of construction company, MACE Ltd.

The partnership's activity centres on 'workplace coordinators'. Their role is to help employers meet their recruiting needs, while providing personalised support for local people, particularly the long-term unemployed, to find work in the construction industry. In addition to their mentoring and coaching role, coordinators also organise formal training towards qualifications and industry standard requirements, such as the Construction Standards Certification Scheme (CSCS).

Since the scheme became fully operational in July 2003, over 250 people have found jobs, while around 850 people have completed valuable construction qualifications. EQUAL has funded six workplace coordinators to work with private developers, local authorities and a housing association on six development sites across London.

Businesses give their support

A key success of the scheme has been the high level of private sector buy-in. Three major developers that are partners have chosen to retain and fund workplace coordinators on their sites now that EQUAL funding has ended. David Rowbotham of MACE Ltd explained what makes the scheme so unique: "*It's a good idea that is being effectively delivered in partnership with the private sector. It's not seen as a government-led initiative which is a refreshing change for us and because workplace coordinators are part of our organisation, the scheme is taken seriously... it's our reputation on the line".*

The popularity and effectiveness of the approach has also seen the partnership win significant public sector backing. At least one London borough has firm plans in place to allocate "Section 106" monies raised from private developers through planning approvals towards supporting the scheme's continuance. Furthermore over €435 000 of co-financing funding from the London Development Agency (LDA) and the European Social Fund has already been secured for unemployed jobseekers registered with the Government's Jobcentre Plus agency to receive training through the programme.

A more detailed version and other EQUAL success stories can be found at: http://europa.eu.int/comm/employment_social/equal/activities/ search_en.cfm

Unemployment was tackled by matching local people to local jobs

Country: United Kingdom
Region: London
Project name: Building London Creating Futures
Project duration: November 2001 – November 2005
ESF priority area: Adaptability
ESF funding (€): 1 798 314
Total funding (€): 5 365 372
National EQUAL partners: 21 partners
Transnational partnership with: France, Germany
Contact details:
London Borough of Southwark
Lisa-Marie Bowles
Regeneration Department
Chiltern House
Portland Street
UK-London SE17 2ES
Tel: +44 20 7525 5486
E-mail: Lisa-Marie.Bowles@southwark.gov.uk
Website: www.buildinglondon.co.uk

Innovation ▶

Mainstreaming

Transnationality

Empowerment ▶

Partnership ▶

Tackling redundancies – coaching the players

Industrial decline has hit the southern region of Wallonia in Belgium hard. Once thriving industries in the steel, coal, textile and printing sectors have been forced to close or to outsource their manufacturing activities so as to compete in the global market. Several thousand employees have lost their jobs as a result, and few employers have been able to offer retraining opportunities or support for reintegration in the labour market.

In the late 1990s, the Walloon regional government responded by creating the "Plans d'Accompagnement des Reconversions" (PAR) – a plan for support services to employees threatened with, or already affected by, collective redundancies. It included the creation of several temporary specialised units – so called "reconversion" units – managed in most cases by the trade unions. They offered services such as personal and professional coaching and guidance on retraining and finding a job.

Despite some encouraging results, the "reconversion" units were criticised for being too "ad-hoc" and lacking an overall strategy to ensure their success. The plan also failed to make sufficient use of existing services available through the public employment service, FOREM.

A more strategic approach to support services

The DECRIRE Development Partnership (DP), set up with support from EQUAL in early 2000, builds directly on the experience of the PAR. It has developed a practical guide on how to set up and manage a "reconversion" unit. This enables new units to be set up quickly and efficiently in response to new threats of redundancies in a particular region or sector. It also ensures that units apply common standards to the services provided, while allowing sufficient flexibility for adaptation of the services to the region or sector's specific needs.

The guide talks through the overall mandate and objectives of a unit, the key partners to involve in its creation, their potential role and functions, and their rights and obligations. It provides concrete advice on coordination of the unit and the development of a strategic work programme. An easy to use checklist helps users to verify, step-by-step, whether all the requirements for the successful creation and operation of the unit have been taken into account. DECRIRE also offers a consultation service to supplement the guide.

DECRIRE has been a huge success. In 2003, 18 "reconversion" units in various sectors (including the textile, construction, glass and transport sectors) were set up in the Walloon region with the help of the new tool and method. These units were able to provide assistance and training to some 4 314 employees at risk or unemployed. Between 60% and 90% of those assisted by the different units were able to find a new job.

New partners work towards a common goal

The success of the DECRIRE DP can be largely attributed to getting the partnership right. The public employment service, FOREM, led the DP as it has direct access to information on job and vocational training opportunities – essential for the services offered by the "reconversion" units. But involvement of the two major Belgian trade unions was critical. In mass redundancies, they are the ones who link directly with those threatened with redundancy. Their participation ensured that the guide emphasises the "human" and social dimension of the units' services. A unit's role is not just to help find a new job or to identify training opportunities, but also to offer a place of solidarity and understanding.

The involvement of smaller, sector-specific employee organisations also provided a useful perspective when developing the guide. And finally academic partners helped to develop the methodology and analysis and have been monitoring application of the guide.

The DECRIRE DP has in fact worked as a kind of "umbrella" organisation, bringing together organisations that have in the past been reluctant to cooperate. EQUAL has shown them the benefits of cooperation.

Widespread promotion reaps its rewards

Given the guide's promising results, the DECRIRE partners have begun to promote it more widely. A toolkit has been developed, including presentations of the guide and its results. It includes a DVD, in which employees facing redundancy describe how they benefited from the services provided through the "reconversion" units. The DVD also includes a visit to a unit, with a commentary on how it is organised and run.

Training for a new job in a marble factory in Nivelles, Belgium

> *"For me taking part in the activities has been a big step forward – a door wide open. When my company closed down, I found out that FOREM offered a range of training opportunities as well as advice on how to find a new job. This support really helped me in this terrible time. That was great. After a few weeks, I felt stronger and much more ready to face new employers. I am now working in a completely new sector, but using the skills I gained in my previous job."*
> One of the beneficiaries of services offered through a "reconversion" unit.

The toolkit has been presented to regional and local politicians, employers, social partners and many others who could potentially benefit from the approach developed by DECRIRE.

The activities of the DP have had a strong political impact. A Decree adopted by the Walloon Region states that workers affected by collective redundancy have the right to benefit from the coaching and support offered by such "reconversion" units. More importantly, it also sets out the procedures for developing and running such units, which directly integrate the tools and guidance developed by the DECRIRE DP. Through this new legal instrument, the "reconversion plan" can now be applied strategically and effectively on the ground. The adoption of this law is the ultimate symbol of DECRIRE's success, and widens its impact to the whole Walloon region.

But DECRIRE is also preparing to go beyond the national borders and its results have been presented at several international events. As a result, DPs from Italy and France have shown a keen interest in the tool and method developed and are currently looking into the possibilities of transferring and adapting these to their own national contexts.

A more detailed version and other EQUAL success stories can be found at: http://europa.eu.int/comm/employment_social/equal/activities/search_en.cfm

Country: Belgium
Region: Wallonia
Project name: DECRIRE
Project duration: 36 months
National partners: FOREM, CAREMPLOI, CEFRET and ULB – Travail Emploi Formation
Transnational partnership: France, Italy
ESF priority area: Adaptability
ESF funding (€): 350 309
Total funding (€): 700 618
Contact details:
FOREM
Anny Poncin
Boulevard Tirou 104
B-6000 Charleroi
Tel: +32 71 206 111
E-mail: anny.poncin@forem.be, info@basta.se
Website: www.leforem.be

Innovation

Mainstreaming

Transnationality

Empowerment

Partnership

Changing systems, changing lives

EQUAL at Work

It is widely accepted that individuals need to be flexible and adaptable to increase their opportunities for employment. But it is more contentious to suggest that organisations need to change to encourage a more diverse and inclusive workforce. While Human Resources (HR) systems are generally considered to be neutral or benign influences in this respect, the "Equal at Work" Development Partnership (DP) has demonstrated that this is not always true.

Work undertaken by the lead organisation in the DP, the Dublin Employment Pact, provided the starting hypothesis for Equal at Work: that HR practices can act to slow or prevent the recruitment and progression of vulnerable groups within the labour market – hampering the move from "doing a job" to "having a career". Crucially, the DP works to alter systems, rather than improving the employability of individuals. As Philip O'Connor, Director of Equal at Work, says: "…So many of our actions focused nearly exclusively on 'employability' over the last few years. It would work to a point, but we could always see the need for organisations and companies to change what they do. EQUAL gave us the chance to take a 'big-bang' approach to changing things."

Working across sectors to remove barriers

Equal at Work aimed to review all aspects of the system – pre-recruitment, recruitment and progression – in the three main sectors of the labour market: private, public, and voluntary. Recognising the differences in HR practices between these sectors was crucial to the transferability of the work: it would be unrealistic to expect a private sector employer to adopt the same approach as the voluntary/community sector.

Actions and solutions have been specific to each sector but the unifying goal remained the same: to develop open and inclusive HR polices and practices, to remove artificial barriers and to promote a more diverse, inclusive and open labour market.

In the public sector, the DP started by reviewing how local authorities recruited new staff. Particular emphasis was placed on entry requirements as they can present significant barriers to people with few qualifications. As a result of EQUAL's involvement, candidates for jobs are now assessed through a more competence-based recruitment system, taking better account of their informal knowledge and skills.

New solutions for the private sector

A job-rotation model was piloted in the private sector after the DP convinced two large firms to take part. By encouraging workers to try out new working environments, habits and tasks, the project helped them to develop additional skills and to gain a better understanding of how the company worked as a whole. The firms, on the other hand, were able to better assign people to tasks and functions they were most suited to. This project has led directly to ten people – many refugees or new migrants – being offered full-time employment. One member of this group had an accountancy qualification from his country of origin and is now studying to gain the equivalent Irish qualifications – with the support of his new employer. The model was recommended for mainstreaming by EQUAL Ireland.

The voluntary and community sector is extremely diverse in terms of themes, size and structures of organisations. The DP wanted to gain a clearer view of their HR systems and processes, and therefore launched a study to identify good practices in this area. Training was then developed to make sure that other voluntary and community organisations could learn from these good practices.

All the actions launched by EQUAL at Work were supported by a cross-cutting working group which concentrated on developing training modules and making the business case for increased equality and diversity in the workplace.

The "demand side" was important in the partnership

In order to carry out such a wide range of activity, partnership has been fundamental to the Equal at Work DP, with nearly 50 organisations from the three sectors involved. Key actors include: two local authorities, a large hospital, five statutory agencies, three trade unions, four employer organisations and networks, eight training/educational bodies, 11 Area Partnership Companies and 14 NGOs or community organisations.

© Dailylife

Claire, an older woman who needed to re-enter work after a long absence caring for her sick husband, was involved in the on-the-job training offered through Equal at Work. She now has a full-time job with a mental health organisation. And "Diane", a young traveller with no secondary education leaving certificate is now employed at Dublin City Council as clerical officer, as a direct result of her participation in the EQUAL project's work experience and training activities.

Major partners in the DP – such as Dublin City Council, private sector companies, voluntary and community organisations – also represented the "demand side" of mainstreaming. They wanted to find out ways to improve their HR methods and, through direct involvement, learnt how to do so in practice.

A more detailed version and other EQUAL success stories can be found at: http://europa.eu.int/comm/employment_social/equal/activities/ search_en.cfm

Country: Ireland
Region: Dublin
Project name: EQUAL at Work – Dublin Employment Pact
Project duration: June 2002 – September 2004
ESF priority area: Adaptability
ESF funding (€): 751 340
Total funding (€): 1 149 375
National EQUAL partners: Dublin Employment Pact and 28 national partners
Transnational partnership with: Northern Ireland, Germany, Spain, Hungary, Poland
Contact details:
Dublin Employment Pact
Mary Bigley
Project Manager, Equal at Work
7 North Great Georges Street
Dublin 1, Ireland
Tel: +353 (0)1 878 8900
E-mail: mbigley@dublinpact.ie
Website: www.dublinpact.ie

The sea is the limit

The fishing industry in the Azores has suffered several serious setbacks over the last decade. The islands are located in the middle of the Atlantic Ocean, and the variety of fish is already limited by extreme depth of the seabed a short distance from the coast. But recent European fishing quotas further restrict the quantity and species of fish that can be caught. Added to this, the islands' harbour infrastructure and fishing fleet are both in urgent need of renovation. Most of the ports lack basic facilities such as cold storage and machinery to lift boats out of the water, and the boats, 80% of which are shorter than 9 metres, lack storage possibilities, decks or cabins.

Largely as a result of these threats, unemployment among fishermen is high, but mostly hidden. Some 85% of all workers in the sector do not (or rather, are unable to) work full-time. The workforce is also ageing fast because the industry is not able to attract young people, so there is a high risk that important skills will be lost. What's more, workers in the fishing industry tend to have very low levels of formal education and training, and efforts to help them update their skills have so far been unsuccessful.

Working with all sectors of the community

The Mudança de Maré Development Partnership (DP) brought together many different organisations and stakeholders to tackle the challenges faced by the Azorean fishing industry. The involvement of local development associations and cooperatives (representing the crew of more than 500 boats) ensured the project's close cooperation with the local fishing community. Youth associations took part to raise young people's awareness of the benefits of working in the fishing industry and to highlight the importance of proper education and training. Two women's rights organisations helped to address the gender issues that characterise the fishing industry – a sector heavily dominated by men and "male customs". A film production company was also invited into the DP to reverse the sector's negative image using film. And last but not least, the participation of the Azorean regional authority for agriculture, fishing and environment ensured the policy relevance of Mudança's activities.

Mudança de Maré had three key goals: modernisation, reorientation, and "valorisation". Its activities were based on an in-depth audit of the sector, taking account of the overall socio-economic situation, the sector's employment profile and new trends and opportunities. Each of the DP's activities were therefore based on real problems and needs rather than perceived ones.

Some 39 activities were carried out, each with a specific aim such as: modernising skills, techniques and infrastructure; helping workers to find alternative ways of making a living in the sector (for example through tourism or alternating fishing methods and species fished); protecting nautical heritage; increasing the levels of confidence and cooperation among workers in the sector; and improving the sector's image.

Getting women on board

A key activity of Mudança de Maré was to develop the existing knowledge and skills of women, and to make them aware of their rights. Generations of women have worked in the fishing industry helping to prepare bait, nets and traps, unload boats, and process the catch. But their contribution has frequently gone unrecognised and they are hardly ever paid for their work.

The EQUAL project organised an 8-month training programme for 12 women from different backgrounds and ages. It combined theoretical courses (including IT, English, administration, health and gender equality) and on-the-job training. Specific emphasis was placed on how to use their new skills in the fishing sector, for example by offering administration and accounting services. It is hoped that in the longer term the women will set up small cooperatives to provide paid services to the fishing sector.

The EQUAL project arranged for the course participants to meet with women from the other islands and to take part in a conference in Spain, so as to exchange experiences and views with women from other fishing communities.

> One participant reported: "*It made me realise that traditions and habits vary enormously in Europe, and even between two islands of the same Archipelago! For example, on our island, it is considered inappropriate for a woman to work – or even set foot sometimes – on a boat. And on the other island (Terceira), just a few kilometres away, women do it all the time, and there are even some that navigate their own boat.*"

The Azores fishing industry is in need of modernisation

A better future through partnership

Mudança de Maré was not the only EQUAL partnership helping the fishery sector to adapt to the demands and trends of the new millennium. Under the "Pêche et Aquaculture transnational partnership", the Azorean DP joined forces with four others in Spain, Italy and France that focused on fishing as their central theme.

Despite sometimes conflicting interests regarding access rights to fishing territories, the exchange of views and experiences enabled the partnership to come up with a series of common recommendations for EU fisheries policy. And on a practical level, Italy's legislation on tourism in the fishery sector inspired Mudança de Maré to recommend changes to their own policies and legislation in this area. As a result, the regional authority has recently proposed new legislation to help the fishing community contribute to the tourism sector, using the Italian approach as a model.

A more detailed version and other EQUAL success stories can be found at: http://europa.eu.int/comm/employment_social/equal/activities/ search_en.cfm

Country: Portugal
Region: Azores
Project name: Mudança de Maré
Project duration: 2 years 10 months
ESF priority area: Adaptability
ESF funding (€): 811 047
Total funding (€): 1 083 896
National EQUAL partners: Associação Crescer em Confiança, Associação Juvenil da Ilha de Santa Maria, Cooperativa de Comercialização Porto de Abrigo, Direcção Regional de Pescas da Secretaria Regional Agricultura Pescas Ambiente, Filmebase, Serviços Cinematográficos, Lda., Terra-Mar Associação para o Desenvolvimento Local nos Açores, UMAR – União de Mulheres Alternativa e Resposta, Vianapesca, O.P. – Cooperativa de Produtores de Peixe de Viana do Castelo, Crl
Transnational partnership with: France, Spain and Italy
Contact details:
Associação Marítima Açoreana (AMA)
Luis Rodrigues
Rua do Pires, 71 Rabo de Peixe
P-9600-123-Rabo de Peixe, Ribeira Grande
Tel: +351 29620 1552/0
E-mail: lrodrigues@pescas.net
Website: www.pescas.net or
www.ajism.org/mm/activ.htm

Innovation

Mainstreaming

Transnationality

Empowerment

Partnership ▶

A new approach to transferring know-how

Like many industrialised countries, France faces the progressive ageing of its population. The trend is expected to worsen over the next few years as birth rates keep dropping and life expectancy continues to rise. In this context, promoting active ageing and policies to foster the employability of the over-50s are priority goals. But the number of people taking part in job-related training in France is low compared to other European countries. Moreover, most training is targeted at young people, with only 3% of training programmes designed for those aged 55-64.

The Part'@ge EQUAL Development Partnership aims to counter this problem by promoting lifelong learning opportunities for senior workers in agriculture, and the milk sector in particular. Its objective is to encourage the transfer of know-how between generations within companies faced by an ageing workforce. The DP analyses the needs of each company and develops an individual training programme for transferring skills. It has pioneered a tutoring system where older and younger workers pool knowledge and skills.

Part'@ge is promoting lifelong learning in the milk sector

© European Community

Age management: looking to the long term

The Development Partnership (DP) is led by the Pierre Mendès-France University in Grenoble and works with a number of companies linked to the French Milk Board in the Rhone-Alps region. "*It is essential to offer to ageing workers the possibility to evolve within the company in order to avoid the loss of valuable skills. It is a matter of adaptability, training and career management,*" explains Marie-Antoinette Blondin, responsible for vocational training in one of the companies.

Nevertheless, dealing with ageing workers is not easy: agricultural companies usually focus on short-term problems like market constraints and falling milk prices, while age management goals have to be seen with a long-term view. Putting in place training activities for senior workers requires good communication strategies, based on strong and convincing arguments. Older workers are often difficult to motivate: they lack confidence to take on new learning possibilities and are sceptical about extending their working life. Some decide to take advantage of early retirement schemes which allow workers to retire before the age of 60.

Training methods adapted to individual needs

Part'@ge developed tailor-made training programmes which were adapted not only to each company, but also to each sector and worker within the company. The training was designed to respond to real needs and use feasible, low-cost learning methods. To fully understand the specific problems of companies and their in-house potential, the DP started with an in-depth analysis of the internal structure and workforce of the four companies taking part. This also took account of the local context, including regional labour market trends, and profiled the workforce, highlighting the added value brought by each worker within the enterprise.

As a result of consultations with managers and employees, Part'@ge understood much better the expectations of both groups, and was able to develop communication and training methods that seamlessly fitted the needs and potential of each company.

Tutoring systems help to transfer know-how between colleagues

At Candia, a milk producer, one technician responsible for running a machine filling cartons was trained as a tutor. With the help of training organised by Part'@ge he was able to build up his own technical know-how, formalise his expertise, and then transfer it to colleagues through a series of workshops. Around a third of the company's employees has now benefited from training under programmes developed by the DP.

Cross-sharing skills between generations

Up to now, most activities aimed at tackling the problem of ageing workers were developed in order to transfer skills from the older generation to the younger one. Part'@ge is reversing this one-sided approach by developing a real and concrete exchange of expertise across generations. The DP has set up a tutoring scheme where younger workers can take advantage of the experience of senior workers while sharing their own knowledge of information technology and new products. This cross-sharing of skills and abilities is aimed at fostering the professional development of workers of both age groups.

By incorporating tailor-made training activities for senior workers, this EQUAL DP has injected a new impulse into a very traditional sector. Activities targeted at senior workers were organised with the specific working context in

mind. Its approach has helped companies face the need to adapt their ageing workforces by making the best use of their own dynamics and resources.

A more detailed version and other EQUAL success stories can be found at: http://europa.eu.int/comm/employment_social/equal/activities/search_en.cfm

Country: France
Region: Rhône-Alpes
Project name: Part'@ge
Project duration: June 2002 – May 2005
ESF priority area: Adaptability
ESF funding (€): 265 766
Total funding (€): 575 045
National EQUAL partners: Université Pierre Mendès-France and 12 others
Transnational partnership with: Belgium, France
Contact details:
UPMF
Bruno Lamotte
1241 Rue des Résidences BP 47
F-38040 Grenoble cedex 9
Tel: +33 476825435
E-mail: bruno.lamotte@upmf-grenoble.fr
Website: www.upmf-grenoble.fr/partage

Innovation

Mainstreaming

Transnationality

Empowerment

Partnership

Validating skills from a distance

Greek SMEs, a high proportion of which are family-based, struggle to survive due to a lack of technical skills and up-to-date knowledge. Training is only accessible to a few, and often bears little relation to actual needs. In addition, the self-employed lack time and resources to invest in extensive training in new skills.

At the same time, those people at risk of exclusion from the jobs market and living in remote areas have no support systems to gain recognition for the skills they possess. Where skills can be validated, the criteria used are often unrelated to labour market demand. Together these factors risk driving SMEs out of business, leaving unemployed people unable to prove their professional skills and experience.

A solution for people in remote areas

The aims of the "Technomatheia" Development Partnership (DP) are twofold: to address the issue of validation of skills in specialised areas (such as car air-conditioning and digital photography) and to match training courses for adults to the job profiles needed in the labour market. The DP also took on board the issue of people living in remote areas seeking solutions through the innovative use of Information and Communication Technologies (ICT). *"Why not reach out to people by bringing the solution closer to them and at the same time develop their ICT skills instead of making them go through bureaucratic procedures which will discourage them to take up training in the first place?"* explains Gerassimos Sourbis, project co-ordinator.

The DP has national coverage and found its roots in the Vocational Training Centre of the Hellenic Confederation of Professionals, Craftsmen and Merchants. Its three main activities were to develop up-to-date training packages in the form of e-learning, validate skills to fit labour market needs through ICT (e-validation), and create accurate job profiles to support the e-learning and e-validation activities.

Traditional validation procedures have long been used in Greece, but neglect people living in remote areas who cannot easily access the central accreditation centres. The ICT-based system developed with the help of EQUAL has created significant opportunities for this group. They can now validate their skills by taking a two-part computer-based exam, including a theoretical part examined by

internet and a practical component examined via video-conferencing. A total of 80 people have so far benefited from the e-validation procedure.

> *"I have been a car air-conditioning technician for 20 years but I could not prove this on paper. E-validation offered me the opportunity to show that I had the skills needed for car air-conditioning work without me having to go through a lot of travelling and time-consuming training courses in order to obtain some kind of qualification"*, says Manolis, who participated in the project.

Matching training to job market needs

To develop new job profiles better suited to labour market needs, the DP cooperated extensively with universities as well as training centres and social partners. Training packages are now being developed for several sectors matching the practical skills needed for specific jobs. The next goal is to feed these profiles into the new e-validation system. The DP has also successfully implemented a new method of job rotation in Greece: employees having to leave the company to take a training course (online or in class) have been replaced by unemployed persons. This form of job rotation benefits three target groups at the same time: the employer, who can ensure continuity of activities within the firm, the employed, who get additional training to increase their potential, and the unemployed, who get on-the-job training while looking for work.

The success of this EQUAL project lies for a great part in its partnership, which brought together a wide range expertise to develop e-learning and e-validation systems corresponding to labour market needs. This also helped to raise the DP's profile with the education and employment ministries.

"This is the first time ever that we succeeded in connecting universities and the Ministry of Education on the one hand and social partners, training and validation institutes and the Ministry of Employment on the other", says Angeliki Athanassouli from the National Accreditation Centre of Greece.

© Getty Image

Improved chances of finding work

Because of this DP's unique partnership, it was possible to bring education and training programmes for adults closer to the needs of the labour market. As a result of this successful cooperation, a Green Paper has been agreed by the social partners and the Ministry of Employment requiring all future training programmes be based on up-to-date job profiles. It means that people following training courses now have a better chance of finding a job afterwards thanks to the improved match between courses offered and the real demands of the labour market.

A more detailed version and other EQUAL success stories can be found at: http://europa.eu.int/comm/employment_social/equal/activities/ search_en.cfm

Country: Greece
Region: Prefectures of Attica, Western Greece, Crete and Central Macedonia
Project name: Technomatheia
Project duration: January 2002 – May 2005
ESF priority area: Adaptability
ESF funding (€): 1 430 668
Total funding (€): 1 907 557
National EQUAL partners: Aristotle University of Thessaloniki; Athens Chambers of Small and Medium Sized Industries; Foundation for Research and Technology Hellas; Greek Manpower Employment Organization; Halkidiki's Development Corporation; Hellenic Institute for Occupational Health – Safety; Hellenic Open University; National Accreditation Centre of Vocational Training Strucrures – A.S.S.; Vocational Training Centre-Institute of Labour-General Confederation of Labour
Transnational partnership with: Germany, Ireland, Italy
Contact details:
Vocational Training Centre of the Hellenic Confederation of SMEs (GSEVEE)
Mr G. Sourbis
Ayon Μελετίon 166
GR-104 45 Athens
Tel: +30 210 8544666
E-mail: equal@kekgsevee.gr
Website: www.kekgsevee.gr
www.technomatheia.gr

Innovation ▶

Mainstreaming ▶

Transnationality

Empowerment

Partnership ▶

Improving the gender balance in politics

Women account for less than 10% of all positions in Italian parliaments and governments, be it at municipal, regional or national level. This is a serious democratic deficit. It means that half of the population is not adequately represented in the decision-making processes that affect all citizens. It also deprives Italy, and the EU as a whole, of a large pool of female talent, and risks leaving women's interests and needs off the policy agenda.

The Development Partnership (DP) Esserci aimed to get a fairer representation of women in Italian politics. It used the run up to the European Elections as a test bed for its strategies, and the results were impressive: the proportion of women elected as Members of the European Parliament (MEPs) in Italy rose from 11.5% in 1999 to 19.2% in 2004.

The Esserci DP was coordinated by Arcidonna, a women's organisation founded in 1986 to promote freedom and equal opportunities for women and to combat gender discrimination. They joined forces with local governments, political parties, trade unions, trade associations, women's NGOs, banks, financial and credit institutions to pave the way for change.

Getting the public ready to embrace change

The project's first step was to conduct a survey on the position of women in society and in government. They found that only 5.3% of all respondents (comprising a sample of around 4 500 people) opposed a more equal representation of women and men in the national Parliament. Furthermore, 18.5% of men, and 30.2% of women said they would react positively to a better gender balance in candidate lists for elections.

The survey results have been fed into an Observatory that maps out women's role in Italian institutions such as the banking sector, trade unions and in different levels of government. Together with its transnational partners in Austria, the Netherlands and Spain, Esserci also created a European Observatory on female presence in decision-making bodies, which continues to operate now the EQUAL project has ended.

Using the survey results and observatory data, the Esserci DP then launched a massive awareness raising campaign, focusing on two key messages. Posters carrying the slogan

"Democrazio. Al maschile è un errore" ("Democracy. In the masculine form, is a mistake") were displayed in Rome, Catania, Palermo and Milan airports for 15 days at the end of 2003. Then the slogans "Democracy needs women" and "More Italian women into the European Parliament" were printed on a fan showing the distribution of seats in the EP.

The extensive media work proved particularly successful. Press conferences were organised across the country, and interviews were broadcast on regional and national television, including prime time news. Several regions participated in the distribution of other promotional materials such as leaflets, stickers, postcards, t-shirts and flags. The campaign won two prizes in Italy: an Agora Silver Award for the best social campaign and an Acorn Award in the Piedmont Region. But most important were its results. The number of women among the Italian MEPs rose from 11% in the previous election, to 19.2% in 2004.

Through its network of women's NGOs across Italy, the DP also cooperated with schools throughout the country, to train students on the issues of citizenship and gender equality. Over 6 000 students, aged 16 to 18, took part in the courses, which included sessions on gender identities, their impact on participation in economical and political life, and EU and national legislation on equal opportunities.

Mainstreaming: making law – making history

The Esserci DP was instrumental in lobbying for improvements to, and compliance with, regional and national legislation on equal access for women and men to public office. In 2003 article 51 of the Italian Constitution was modified and now provides for positive action to promote equal opportunities between women and men. In 2004, the Italian Minister of Equal Opportunities for Women and Men introduced a new bill into the legislative process, requiring that one third of candidates must be women. This new provision brought support from women from all political parties, but the outcome is yet to be decided. Networking, campaign tools and methods developed by Esserci are helping to increase public pressure on parliamentarians.

At a regional level, Arcidonna challenged the under-representation of women on candidate lists in court. Its proposal to have a man-woman-man-woman distribution (the so-called zip system) on all lists for local, provincial and

regional elections opened a debate in the Sicilian Regional Parliament. Thanks to the political activity of Arcidonna and its allies, the Sicilian electoral law has been modified and combines a zip system for majority votes with the requirement that both women and men must be represented by at least 30% of the candidates on parties' lists for proportional representation.

"*Women have become protagonists of the long journey towards modern democracy. In the new perspective of development and growth linked to social change, they represent a valuable resource to support the process of renewal and progress*". The Secretary General of the Presidency Gaetano Gifuni in a public address in 2003, in which he also conveyed the "warm support" of the President of the Republic for Arcidonna's initiative.

A more detailed version and other EQUAL success stories can be found at: http://europa.eu.int/comm/employment_social/equal/activities/ search_en.cfm

Country: Italy
Region: National
Project name: Esserci
Project duration: 3 years 2 months
ESF priority area: Equal opportunities
ESF funding (€): 727 558
Total funding (€): 1 455 117
National EQUAL partners: 13 organisations
Transnational partnership with:
Austria, Spain, the Netherlands
Contact details:
Arcidonna
Valeria Ajovalsit, President
Via Alessio di Giovanni 14
I-90144 Palermo
Tel: +39 091 345799
E-mail: valeria.ajovalsit@arcidonna.it
Website: www.arcidonna.org

Making the city a better place to live and work

Like many European cities, Prato, in Italy's Tuscany region, is having to adjust to economic and social change. Most local employers are small or micro enterprises in traditional industry sectors such as textiles. To compete in the global market, they are required to be ever more flexible to respond to fluctuating demands. Employees, meanwhile, find it difficult to cope with irregular or atypical working hours, because they do not coincide with the availability of services such as childcare, schools, shops and stores, and even public transport.

Reconciling working time with citizens' private and family needs is one of the key issues being addressed within the municipality's multi-annual action plan, which was set up to respond to challenges linked to the reorganisation of production systems and its impact on the labour market. In this context the city established a "Time Agency" (Consulta permanente degli Orari e dei Tempi della citta), which helps people, and predominantly women, to balance jobs with care and other family tasks.

The "time lab" – a community service

The Laboratorio del tempo Development Partnership (DP) was launched by the Prato Time Agency, in cooperation with the municipality, a large employers' consortium and the University of Florence. Together they designed a "time lab" consisting of a local resource centre and a series of pilot actions implemented in companies and public administrations.

The local resource centre provides a wide range of services for both women and men of all age groups and from different life situations. For instance, baby-sitting and childcare services, available in the afternoon when kindergartens and schools are closed, became a lifeline for parents with irregular working times. Entrepreneurship training and courses in ICT, Internet use, knowledge management and foreign languages were set up to meet the needs of various target groups, always including the offer of childcare. ICT courses attracted greatest demand, since these skills are critical for today's labour market. These courses brought together the old and young – many become "regulars" in the Laboratorio's much frequented Internet Café.

Other services focused on providing family support to young parents. A key priority was to overcome gender stereotyping and encourage men to share in household duties or care tasks. This included, for example, a course entitled "S.O.S – Il Casalingo" (SOS Male-Household) which trained men in household tasks, such as ironing, cooking, washing and cleaning. Most participants not only acquired new skills, but also came to value the unpaid work of women in the home.

Creative solutions from employers

The DP's cooperation with CONSER, an employers' consortium with a membership of 300 small and micro enterprises, has been particularly beneficial to the local workforce. Together, these companies employ more than 3 000 people, predominantly in the textile sector. CONSER has already helped its members to introduce changes that have environmental benefits, such as a water recycling and energy saving system, and recruitment of a joint "mobility manager". Participation in this EQUAL project enabled the consortium to turn its attention to improving the work-life balance of their employees.

A detailed analysis of the situation revealed that considerable time was being lost in carrying out daily routines. As Pierpaolo Dettori, CONSER's Mobility Manager, explains: "*We found that, on average, of the 3 000 employees working here, 1 000 go every day to the supermarket, to the dry cleaners, the post office or to take their kids to school and 2 400 drive to work in their own cars causing regular traffic jams.*" CONSER therefore decided to set up its own transport service. Using 10 electric vans

Childcare services allow parents more flexible working hours

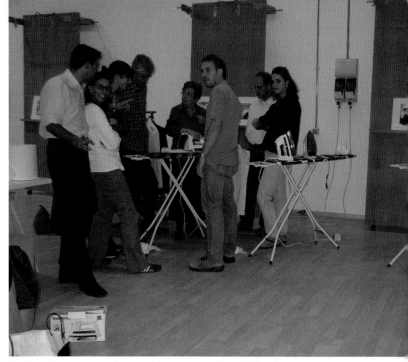

Men have been very receptive to training courses on household tasks

donated by the city, employees were able to travel in groups and at times when there is less traffic congestion. This new mode of commuting was only possible because the companies involved harmonised their working hours to fit in with the transport schedules.

Another joint venture with the municipality involved the creation of a childcare centre with opening hours adapted to the working times of parents. The city provided a piece of land free of charge, and CONSER is now investing in the construction of a new building to house the care facility. In addition, to make the lives of working parents a lot easier, postal services have been set up in the zone and centralised laundry and shopping services are being established.

A lasting impact – in Prato and beyond

Thanks to the involvement and commitment from the municipality and employers, the DP's initiatives will bring about lasting change in the city of Prato. The "Laboratorio del tempo" community centre, for example, has now become a permanent institution, managed and financed by the municipality. And after assessing its costs and benefits, several of the larger participating companies decided to fund part of the running costs of the transport service.

But the EQUAL project's impact is also being felt beyond the city's boundaries. Says Christina Pugi, the project director of the Laboratorio del Tempo DP: "*Through visibility events and networks our good practices have been disseminated beyond the partnership. Social, political, economic, cultural and civic institutions that are interested in bringing about change in the city and in the perception of the gender roles of its citizens are adopting our approaches. We are also receiving additional EQUAL funding to multiply and mainstream the Laboratorio model outside the Tuscany region and even outside Italy.*"

Collaboration with partners in France and Spain has also produced some interesting results. For example, the Laboratorio del Tempo imported a training scheme developed in Spain that had proved to be successful in supporting women in the creation of small or micro enterprises. The French DP, on the other hand, showcased Prato's household management courses for men in Rennes and is now planning similar activities.

A more detailed version and other EQUAL success stories can be found at: http://europa.eu.int/comm/employment_social/equal/activities/ search_en.cfm

Country: Italy
Region: Tuscany
Project name: Prato: Il Laboratorio del tempo
Project duration: 3 years
ESF priority area: Equal opportunities
ESF funding (€): 783 911
Total funding (€): 1 802 996
National EQUAL partners: ASTIR, CONSER, Comune di Prato – Assessorato alle Pari Opportunita, La Cooperativa delle donne
Transnational partnership with: France, Spain
Contact details:
PIN S.C.R.L., Servizi Didattici e Scientifici per L'Università di Firenze
Cristina Pugi
Piazza Ciardi 25
I-59100 Prato
Tel: +39 0574 602578
E-mail: cristina.pugi@pin.unifi.it
Website: www.laboratoriodeltempo.org/

Set to make a difference

Fewer than 10% of working women in the United Kingdom hold jobs in SET, or in other words, in Science, Engineering and Technology. For the EQUAL Development Partnership (DP) JIVE this figure highlights not only a major lack of equal opportunities for women in these growth sectors, but also the fact that employers are missing out on talents and skills that are urgently needed to boost productivity and innovation in the UK.

Led by the Let's Twist Initiative, (Let's Train Women In Science and Technology) based at both Bradford College and the Sheffield Hallam University, JIVE has forged a powerful coalition of women's training centres, employers' organisations from the most segregated sectors of the labour market, mainstream training and educational institutions, careers services and the National Equal Opportunities Commission.

Regional hubs: a source of innovation

Working together for the first time, these partners created a network of regional "Desegregation Hubs". Three such regional "hubs" have been established in the South-East, Yorkshire & Humber, and Wales, offering a range of services that aim to open up career paths for women in male domains of the labour market and to help employers establish a more diverse workforce.

One of their activities, for example, has been to train higher education staff working in the fields of engineering, construction or technology. Used to dealing with

large groups of male students, lecturers and trainers are often ill equipped to tackle issues that arise when women enter such a learning environment. The new gender equality courses help participants to understand the need for gender inclusive learning and to acquire skills to encourage, support and coach female students.

Partnerships generate widespread interest

At national level the JIVE DP has established partnerships that guarantee a long-term commitment to achieving gender equality across sectors where women are under-represented.

A national mentoring scheme achieved great success, for example. Developed in cooperation with a national women's organisation specialised in women's training and education and gender equality, the scheme operated in schools, learning providers and enterprises. Its basic philosophy was to create a "learning partnership" between the mentor and the mentee. Each mentor was selected on the basis of her capacity to act as a role model for a less experienced woman.

Given the huge demand for the scheme across the country, JIVE created the position of "super mentors". These women were trained by the DP to build and coordinate regional mentoring networks and to supervise other mentors in their area.

Cooperation with the Engineering Construction Industry Training Board (ECITB) also proved fruitful. Given alarming projections of skills gaps, the ECITB is seeking to integrate gender equality and diversity into its largest training programme, the National Apprenticeship Scheme for Engineering Construction. With JIVE's support, the ECITB's training organisation has set up support networks and mentoring for women apprentices. Taster weeks for school students, tested under EQUAL, are also now becoming regular events. And nearly all the training board's personnel including senior managers, head office administrators and field staff have received gender equality training.

Other Industrial Training Boards are now following ECITB's example. Let's Twist, as the "mother organisation" of JIVE and now increasingly the regional hubs, are experiencing a growing demand for gender and diversity training, particularly from work-based training providers.

JIVE: Challenging gender stereotypes in the labour market

The gender and diversity audit called "Culture Analysis Tool" (CAT) developed by JIVE and piloted with ECITB companies has been well received. According to Project Manager Ros Wall, "*CAT not only delivers the analysis of recruitment processes, training environments and working practices, but also functions as a catalyst for discussion around any change needed within the organisation. Thanks to EQUAL, such change processes could then be further supported by JIVE.*"

Steering the gender equality agenda

The involvement of the national Equal Opportunities Commission (EOC) ensured that JIVE achievements contributed to relevant policy priorities. Indeed many of the EOCs recommendations on eliminating labour market segregation are inspired by the work of JIVE. And with support from EQUAL, the EOC is now leading, together with JIVE, a national information campaign to encourage young women to consider a career in engineering, construction, information technology or the craft sector.

Another major achievement is the opening of a National Resource Centre for Women's Training in Science, Engineering and Technology in February 2005. Its mission is to promote best practice in the recruitment, retention and progression of women in SET and the built environment by providing information and advisory services to all key actors. The Centre has a central role in driving forward the UK government's strategy to increase the number of women in SET.

Participation in two transnational partnerships also proved immensely important to the impact of the JIVE DP. For example, in a common effort with the German partner, JIVE used its mentoring model to develop a good practice manual and European guidelines for mentoring and careers guidance. The transnational activity has not only facilitated exchange of ideas and best practice, but

also served to raise the profile of the DP partners, and strengthen their influence on decision-makers.

A more detailed version and other EQUAL success stories can be found at: http://europa.eu.int/comm/employment_social/equal/activities/search_en.cfm

Country: United Kingdom
Regions: Wales, London, Scotland, South East, Yorkshire & Humberside
Project name: JIVE
Project duration: May 2002 – November 2005
ESF priority area: Equal opportunities
ESF funding (€): 4 750 337
Total funding (€): 13 994 611
National EQUAL partners: Oxford Women's Training Scheme, Sheffield Hallam University, The Open University, The Women's Workshop
Transnational partnership with: Germany, France, Finland, Denmark
Contact details:
JIVE (Joint Interventions Partners)
Ros Wall
Department of Engineering & Construction,
Bradford College
Great Horton Road
UK-Bradford, West Yorkshire, BD7 1 AY
Tel: +44 (0) 1274 433355
E-mail: R.Wall@shu.ac.uk
Website:www.jivepartners.org.uk
National Resource Centre for Women's Training in Science, Engineering and Technology:
www.setwomenresource.org.uk
National information campaign:
www.knowyourplace.org.uk

"*This is a time when government and others are recognising the importance of addressing the equality, stereotyping and segregation agenda for the success of their vocational skills programme and for individual success. We believe that the products of JIVE can support positive change in culture and practice and reduce occupational segregation. We hope to help in the process of joining the key delivery agencies with JIVE products and services so that good equality and anti-stereotyping practice is built into mainstream provision as the norm.*" Ann Madden, representative of the EOC in the EQUAL partnership.

Men taking the lead

Employment patterns for women and men in the Netherlands reflect the male breadwinner model. Men work full-time throughout their lives and have little time to spare for looking after the kids. Women tend to work full-time until they become mothers but then start working part-time or leave the labour market altogether. Even if recent research shows things are starting to change, the bulk of the work in Dutch households still seems to fall on female shoulders.

The "Journey along cultures" Development Partnership (DP), coordinated by the Ministry of Social Affairs and Employment, aimed to create more employment opportunities for women by focusing most of its activities on men. The message conveyed through a huge media campaign was clear and simple – "*If more men were prepared to become more involved with tasks in the home, more women would be able to reconcile family and working life.*"

A nationwide audience

Lasting a year and a half, the DP's professional media campaign with the slogan of "Who does what?" has stimulated a lot of attention and also kick-started a national debate in the Netherlands. Three months after its launch, 55% of the Dutch population was aware of the campaign. It included commercials on TV and radio, press conferences, a website (www.wiedoetwat.nl), talk show and several one-off events.

Men were involved in the earliest planning stages, resulting in a tone that was light and humorous appealing to the widest possible male audience.

TV commercials were used initially to confront men with the excuses that they offer to avoid taking on more tasks at home. For instance, one of the adverts showed a man playing golf and claiming that this enabled him to network with peers and advance his career. It was too bad that his golf ambitions prevented him from picking up the kids at the childcare centre but, of course, he could rely on his wife to bring them home.

Getting the positive message across

The next step in the campaign was to concentrate more on motivation and inspiration rather than provocation by addressing some of the cultural dilemmas encountered by both men and women. Whilst women may like the idea of their partners taking on tasks at home, they can often get frustrated when these tasks are performed in a typically "male" way. Similarly, employers are often unenthusiastic about male employees taking on extra family responsibilities. Radio and TV commercials were used to portray the fun and satisfaction that men gain from spending quality time with their kids and the difference that this can make to the lives of their children and partners.

The website was an important communication tool. It provides factual information on relevant legislation and financial regulations and good practices from daily life. With its polls, e-cards and popular games such as "vacuum victim" and "how to dream up a good excuse", it is attracting more and more visitors who keep disseminating the messages.

Men were encouraged by the campaign to start a dialogue on the division of family tasks with their employers and also with colleagues and friends. With the project's assistance, this has resulted in many men making "role sharing agreements" with their partners and/or employers.

> "*It takes guts to leave an important business meeting early and say you have to pick up your daughter from childcare,*" said one father, but the role sharing agreement he negotiated with his boss made things a lot easier and also helped the company develop a positive image as an equal opportunities employer.

Employers are crucial

Joining forces with enterprises was the key to mainstreaming the DP's idea about role sharing agreements in the business world. After all, men seeking to play a more proactive role as fathers and homemakers need more flexible working time arrangements instead of rigid full-time schedules. Companies that supported the DP's action developed awareness raising strategies that stimulated their male employees to consider a more even distribution of care and other family tasks. The DP also cooperated closely with Dutch business schools. With the support of the project, they have now included the topic of role sharing in major business conferences and their management training.

Through NGOs, such as "Milli Görüs" – a Turkish social and religious movement – and the Foundation for the Participation of Turks in the Netherlands, the DP reached out to ethnic minority groups and the issue of role sharing has even been raised in Mosques during Friday afternoon prayers. This has triggered passionate discussions about male and female role patterns in immigrant communities, particularly amongst young people.

Shaping the attitudes of tomorrow

Targeting the future generation of parents was another major concern. This involved discussion forums in schools using a TV talk show format prepared by the DP. Young men and women negotiated on the division of family tasks, and the traditional career guidance process was expanded to include advice and suggestions about combining work, looking after young children and social involvement.

Implementing a mainstreaming strategy from early on was the key to generating lasting change. Companies, schools, sports clubs, cultural associations and grassroots groups are now continuing many of the activities initiated by EQUAL.

"*At the end of the day,*" says Project Director Marjan Jellema, "*we did not change the world in just one and a half years. But our mainstreaming strategy has succeeded in triggering change – even if it will take time until it develops its full impact.*"

A more detailed version and other EQUAL success stories can be found at: http://europa.eu.int/comm/employment_social/equal/activities/ search_en.cfm

Country: the Netherlands (National coverage)
Project name: Reis langs culturen: landen leren van elkaar (Journey along cultures)
Project duration: May 2002 – November 2004
ESF priority area: Equal opportunities
ESF funding (€): 4 988 305
(declared costs for actions 2 & 3)
Total funding (€): 9 976 610
(declared costs for actions 2 & 3)
National EQUAL partners: CINOP, Nederlands Instituut voor Zorg en Welzijn (NIZW)
Transnational partnership with: Germany, Italy
Contact details:
Ministerie van Sociale Zaken
en Werkgelegenheid
Marjan Jellema
Postbus 90801
NL-2509 LVs Gravenhage
Tel: +31 (70) 333 444
E-mail: mjellema@minszw.nl
Website: www.minszw.nl

Innovation

Mainstreaming

Transnationality

Empowerment

Partnership

Gender goes mainstream

The Austrian region of Styria has experience in promoting gender equality in the labour market. A local "Pact for Employment" binds the regional government and employment services to jointly plan labour market policies and incorporates gender mainstreaming as a guiding principle. But this approach has not yet encouraged a sustainable process of gender mainstreaming. An EQUAL-funded Development Partnership found that even where specific gender equality goals were formulated, these usually did not impact on the daily practices of the various players involved in the delivery of employment policies.

Coordinated by a non-profit organisation for regional development and with major input from a regional gender equality association, "Just GeM" set out to make gender equality an integral part of labour market policies in Styria, so that women and men could benefit equally.

A model for mainstreaming

The project developed a six-stage model enabling the key players to look at every step in the process of mainstreaming of policies, from their design to their evaluation. It starts with a gender impact assessment to find out how men and women are represented in the relevant decision-making processes and how they benefit from various training and employment policies. Based on the outcome, gender equality targets are formulated and a viable action plan is developed to attain them.

During the implementation of the action plan, the gender dimension must be integrated into the management and control systems of each organisation. Finally, monitoring and evaluation mechanisms measure the progress achieved as compared to the situation at departure and the agreed targets.

To apply the model to all relevant institutions, the DP trained "gender agents" to initiate and manage the mainstreaming process within their own organisations. The aim was to create a group of in-house experts dedicated to introducing and coordinating the necessary changes.

Agents for change

As a result, pilot projects launched by the new gender agents have been mushrooming in Styria. Municipalities are carrying out gender impact analyses of their services and embarking on gender budgeting to secure a fairer distribution of funding and subsidies in selected policy areas.

The city of Graz, for instance, developed tools and guidelines for gender mainstreaming in sports and family policies. "*This training programme was a real asset,*" says Martin Haidvogl, the Director of Administration, "*thanks to our new gender agent, we can now ensure that employees who are responsible for planning and implementing the various measures acquire the necessary skills. We are also producing a handbook to help other municipalities to apply gender mainstreaming to all areas of local policies.*"

In addition, the regional branch of the Austrian Trade Union Confederation analysed the gender impact of a number of collective agreements and provided training to help works councils identify and eliminate gender discrimination in the workplace. At the same time, the Association of Styrian Innovation Centres and Business Parks is working to incorporate a gender dimension into their members' services and infrastructures.

Benchmarking progress

To measure progress on a regular basis, Just GeM constructed gender equality indicators that are being used in a benchmarking system called Gender Radar. This system presents the levels of gender equality achieved in crucial areas such as education and training, employment and decision-making in the different districts of Styria. It enables comparisons to be made between districts and between different policy areas while measuring progress over time.

The visibility of their gender equality performance has led local decision-makers to become more conscious of their own policies and practices and the gender gaps they still need to tackle. As a result, both the six-stage model developed by Just GeM and the training programme for gender agents are now in great demand.

Partnership was key

The DP feels that the EQUAL partnership approach was the most important success factor in moving towards gender mainstreaming. Just GeM forged a coalition of all the policy makers in a position to turn its ambitious goals into reality, bringing together the regional government, the regional employment office, social partners, chambers of commerce, local municipalities and the region's largest charity.

Gender mainstreaming is a major challenge but the process has taken root in Styria. A second round EQUAL project is now dedicated to further mainstreaming and the authorities and agencies that have benefited from Just GeM's activities are taking a much more pro-active role in this new DP. Building on their experiences of introducing gender mainstreaming, they will train and support other peers to follow suit. For instance, municipalities will coach their counterparts in other Austrian regions and the Styrian branch of the Austrian Trade Union Federation will team up with other regional branches and its headquarters in Vienna.

Companies can use untapped potential

In addition, private companies, including market leaders, have come to recognise the added-value of gender mainstreaming. Facing skills gaps due to demographic changes, they are now eager to use the untapped potential of women and are aware that this requires more than just opportunities for part-time work. In the framework of the new EQUAL project and with the support of in-house gender agents, they will develop work-life balance policies for their employees, gender fair recruitment, selection and career development procedures and initial training for young women and men in those occupations where they are under-represented. Thus, thanks to EQUAL, gender mainstreaming is also being transferred from the public to private sector in this Austrian region.

A more detailed version and other EQUAL success stories can be found at: http://europa.eu.int/comm/employment_social/equal/activities/ search_en.cfm

© Dailylife

Country: Austria
Region: Styria
Project name: Just GeM
Project duration: September 2002 – September 2005
ESF priority area: Equal opportunities
ESF funding (€): 975 112
Total funding (€): 1 950 223
EQUAL national partners: Regionalentwicklungsverein Graz u.Graz Umgebung/ Regionalmanagement Graz u.Graz-U and 30 others
Transnational partnership with: Spain, Italy, the Netherlands
Contact details:
NOWA
Heide Cortolezis
Rudolf-Hans-Bartsch-Straße 15–17
A–8042 Graz
Tel: +43 316/48-26-00/23
E-mail: cortolezis@nowa.at
Website: www.justgem.at

Innovation

Mainstreaming ▶

Transnationality ▶

Empowerment

Partnership ▶

Overcoming gender blindness in careers guidance

Most people in Denmark believe that equal opportunities for women and men already exist in their country. The female employment rate stands at over 80%, indicating that there are hardly any barriers to women's access to the job market. However, a closer look at the statistics reveals huge gender gaps in different sectors and occupations and a disproportionably low number of women in senior positions. Similar divisions exist in education, where girls and boys tend to choose highly traditional career paths. It appears that despite the country's long-standing gender equality policies and legislation, disparities remain, with gender stereotypes at their root.

Led by the Danish Research Centre on Gender Equality at Roskilde University, the EQUAL Development Partnership (DP) "Unge, køn og karriere" (Youth, Gender and Career) set out to widen the vocational choices of women and men – and break the strong gender segregation in the jobs market. The project focused on the crucial years in the lives of young people when dreams about future careers turn into more concrete plans. Careers advisors and teachers in primary and lower secondary schools were targeted along with parents as groups that play an important role during this period.

Careers advisors are key actors

To start with, the project wanted to establish a sound knowledge basis about how careers counselling was provided and the impact that it made. The DP therefore carried out two major surveys: one looking into the practices of careers advisors and the other assessing the experiences of young women and men within the Danish school guidance system.

On the basis of the studies, the project developed a training programme for careers advisors and teachers – aiming to raise their awareness of the gender dimension in their work and improve their knowledge of factors leading to occupational segregation. Implemented throughout the country in 2003 and 2004, the programme attracted a large number of participants. Counsellors presented their own cases and discussed these in the light of the DP's research.

Whilst a fairly high degree of understanding concerning women's interests in non-traditional occupations emerged, a lot of mental blocks were discovered when it came to offering career paths in traditional female domains to young men. The group discussions stimulated further reflection on the nature of male employment in the future as many traditional male jobs, particularly in industry, are threatened by globalisation.

Promoting family discussion

In parallel, the EQUAL project ran courses for parents of students in years 7-10 of lower secondary school. These were organised in cooperation with school counsellors and teachers and provided parents with information on current and future job market perspectives, with the aim of stimulating them to become less stereotyped in their thinking about educational choices. Before the course, pupils brought home a form to be filled in separately by the child and his or her parents, with the idea of triggering a "family discussion" about the pupil's future. This was followed-up during the course when parents were encouraged to think about their child's career aspirations as compared to their own expectations. Parents responded very positively to this method, which often generated an ongoing dialogue at home.

From the earliest stages of planning and scheduling its activities, the DP aimed to have an influence on planned government reforms to streamline the Danish career guidance system. This policy debate seemed to be an ideal opportunity to encourage gender mainstreaming. Consequently, the DP sought to influence both the legislation process and the planned creation of new guidance centres, as well as the future training of careers advisors.

> For years, gender equality had not been an issue in the context of guidance and counselling. "In 2002," explains Aase Rieck-Sörensen, "things began to move. With emerging skills gaps caused by demographic changes, both the careers counsellors and the Ministry of Education showed a growing interest in developing the potential of all young people, and hence, in adopting a new gender sensitive approach, which makes it possible."

In December 2003, the Minister of Education brought together a number of experts and stakeholders to participate in an ongoing "Dialogue Forum" to inspire and fol-low the development and implementation of the reform. Two partners in the EQUAL DP – the Research Centre on Gender Equality and the Danish University of Education – were nominated to join the forum.

Integrating the gender dimension in careers guidance

At the same time, the DP's events helped provoke a broad debate on gender and career choices which brought a bottom-up influence to bear on the decision-making process. As a result, a gender dimension is now firmly enrooted in the reformed Danish careers guidance system. The Education Ministry is one of the partners in a new EQUAL project to extend the focus of gender and guid-ance by including ethnicity, building on the first round EQUAL outcomes. It has also formed an inter-ministerial working group to report on concrete proposals to over-come gender segregation in education and career choic-es, as well as the labour market.

The DP feels it has particularly benefited particularly from new methods developed by transnational partners, under the EQUAL Voices partnership involving other projects from Austria, Finland, Spain and the UK. "*The learning process helped us all to develop a better understanding of the concept of gender mainstreaming and of the continu-ing need for specific actions for women and, in many cases, also for men,*" concludes Aase Rieck-Sörensen, one of the project managers.

A more detailed version and other EQUAL success stories can be found at: http://europa.eu.int/comm/employment_social/equal/activities/ search_en.cfm

Country: Denmark
Project name: Unge, køn og karriere (Youth, gender and career)
Project duration: November 2001 – November 2004
ESF priority area: Equal opportunities
ESF funding (€): 293 151
Total funding (€): 586 375
National EQUAL partners:
The Danish Research Centre on Gender Equality, Center for Ungdomsforskning, Danmarks Pædagogiske Institut, Wolthers Consult
Transnational partnership with:
Austria, Finland, Spain, UK
Contact details:
Centre for Ligestillingsforskning
Aase Rieck-Sörensen & Sine Lehn
Universitetsparken 1, CAT-bygningen
DK-4000 Roskilde
Tel: +45 46742990
E-mail: ars@celi.dk
Website: www.unge-karriere.socialfonden.net

Innovation

Mainstreaming

Transnationality

Empowerment

Partnership

Making asylum seekers more visible

Since 2002, asylum seekers in Finland have been allowed to start work three months after arriving in the country. But finding a job is difficult without a good knowledge of Finnish. And in a homogeneous society like Finland, discrimination is common, especially in the labour market. It can take several months or even years before asylum seekers receive a decision on their asylum applications, meaning a long time spent waiting without any kind of active occupation.

The Becoming Visible Development Partnership (DP) set out to meet this challenge by providing asylum seekers with different learning and employment opportunities – such as language and vocational training – with the aim of helping them become self-sufficient during their stay in Finland. A second objective was to test and share different training tools and approaches. And another important part of its work has been to tackle discrimination by educating the public about the problems facing asylum seekers and increasing their visibility and acceptance in the local community.

> Päivi Sinkkonen, project coordinator at the Tampere Reception Centre, a project partner explains: "Asylum seekers are not the only target group of the DP. There is also a need to challenge attitudes and educate the Finnish public as well as the media, who are often misinformed about asylum seekers."

The DP has helped asylum seekers make the most of the time they spend in Finland while waiting for a decision on their asylum applications. Thanks to the project, over 1 000 asylum seekers were able to take Finnish language classes and other useful courses, such as computer training, metal and woodwork and handicrafts. Practical courses providing an introduction to Finnish culture and society and life management skills were also organised.

Helping employers help asylum seekers

An important part of the DP's work has been helping asylum seekers find employment. Contacts were made with employers in order to organise study visits and practical work placements. Over 100 asylum seekers were able to participate in such placements. The DP also organised an employment fair where asylum seekers had the chance to meet employers and learn about job openings. This also allowed employers to meet and interview potential new employees.

To address the obstacle of employers' lack of knowledge about the legal and administrative procedures for hiring asylum seekers, the DP provided information to both parties on labour law and workers' rights and duties. They also assisted with contacts with trade unions, tax and employment offices and other authorities.

But asylum seekers are not the only beneficiaries of the project. The DP also aims to develop the professional skills of refugee reception centre staff and educate the local community. Training has been provided for staff on the principles of teaching and learning, using pedagogical tools, group coordination and facilitation, the use of drama techniques and multicultural communication.

Mainstreaming has been an important part of the Becoming Visible DP's work. The sharing of good practice (such as participatory teaching methods and organisation of employment fairs) has helped other reception centres and organisations working with asylum seekers develop new work methods.

Visibility and participation lead to acceptance

The DP has succeeded in making asylum seekers "more visible" by organising activities bringing attention to their plight and creating contacts with wider society. These have included events such as a touring photo exhibition, fashion show, football match, and participation in a concert organised by an anti-racism network. These helped involve the local community and put Finns in contact with asylum seekers, while attracting a lot of media interest. In the long run this should make it easier for asylum seekers to be accepted in Finnish society and eventually find jobs.

The DP has also made contact with the Ombudsman for Minorities and Members of Parliament to inform them of legislative gaps and ask them to address issues and problems faced by asylum seekers in Finland. In this way the DP was successful in bringing attention to policies which hinder the job search for asylum seekers, such as ID requirements when opening a bank account and the fact

Having found work, asylum seekers can preparing for a better future

that foreign driving licences expire just one year after a person enters Finland.

In its first phase, four reception centres for asylum seekers located in different parts of Finland participated in the project, in collaboration with the Finnish Association of Adult Education Centres (KTOL). Now in its second phase, the DP has a new name to express the commitment to build on what has been achieved so far: Becoming More Visible. In addition, new partners have joined after learning about the excellent results of the first round.

A more detailed version and other EQUAL success stories can be found at: http://europa.eu.int/comm/employment_social/equal/activities/ search_en.cfm

Country: Finland
Region: Satakunta and Pirkanmaa in South-Western and Central Finland
Project name: Becoming More Visible
Project duration: January 2002 – November 2004
ESF priority area: Asylum seekers
ESF funding (€): 650 773
Total funding (€): 1 301 545
National EQUAL partners: Joutsenon vastaanot-tokeskus, Kansalais- ja työväenopistojen liitto, Perniön vastaanottokeskus, Punkalaitumen vas-taanottokeskus, Tampereen vastaanottokeskus, Turun vastaanottokeskus
Transnational partnership with: Denmark, UK
Contact details:
Finnish Red Cross Southwest District
Pauli Heikkinen, Project Manager
Yliopistonkatu 24A 14
FIN-20100 Turku
Tel: +358 2 274 5541
E-mail: pauli.heikkinen@becomingmorevisible.net
Website: www.becomingmorevisible.net

Innovation

Mainstreaming

Transnationality

Empowerment

Partnership

EQUAL Success stories

Partnership benefits asylum seekers and employers

Officially asylum seekers can work in Spain but it is not easy for them to access the job market. Firstly they need a work permit, which they can only apply for six months after lodging an asylum application. It may then take several months to come through, and even then is only valid for a specific duration and job. Secondly asylum seekers' existing qualifications are often not recognised in Spain. These obstacles contribute to a general reluctance among employers to hire asylum seekers, despite the fact that some sectors face labour shortages.

Accessing the job support network

The ENEAS EQUAL Development Partnership (DP) was set up to help asylum seekers gain useful skills and find work. The partnership has established new forms of cooperation between the public and private sectors. It brings together public administrations from all levels – national, regional, and local – with employers and non-governmental organisations specialised in providing support for asylum seekers.

Asylum seekers access the project through many different channels including asylum centres and the Red Cross. They are referred to different organisations depending on their specific needs – assistance with job search, language or vocational training, etc. As the ENEAS-EQUAL DP covers all of Spain, the project established regional partnerships to take account of the local context and the different service providers active in each area. Employer organisations were among the key partners. They were able to provide training placements through their members, and helped to convince them of the benefits of hiring asylum seekers. Asylum seekers were therefore supported in finding work in various different sectors including tourism, agriculture, manufacturing, building and the service sector.

Opening doors to jobs in tourism

The Spanish Federation of the Hotel and Restaurant Industry (FEHR), for example, was one of the partners. There is a growing demand for qualified staff in the hospitality sector, and asylum seekers often bring linguistic skills that are a great asset to employers. A so called "collaboration agreement" was established between the FEHR and the Spanish Commission for Assistance to Refugees (CEAR). Together they developed a training programme that combines modules such as language classes, dealing with clients and mediation. CEAR was responsible for selecting course participants and teaching the vocational training modules. The FEHR coordinated job interviews and acted as an intermediary between the asylum seeker and employers. On completion of the training programme, participants received an internationally recognised qualification that gives access to more qualified work, and can still be used in the event of repatriation.

Another such collaboration agreement was set up between the Reception Centres for Refugees (CAR) in Seville, the regional department for training and employment and Andalucia Orienta, a regional authority providing vocational training and promoting self-employment. In addition to participating in vocational training programmes, selected asylum seekers have the chance to carry out an internship in companies. This enabled employers to get to know the asylum seeker personally, and has helped to increase awareness and promote intercultural exchange in the wider society.

A win-win situation

The results are impressive. Most of the asylum seekers that have participated in the training programmes went on to find jobs. It also helped people previously working in the black economy to find legal work. Usually these jobs are more visible and of better quality, giving asylum seekers a better chance of integrating into society and making their own living. The effect on employers is also encouraging. According to Carlos Peláez, ENEAS coordinator, "*the better people get to know asylum seekers, and the less they confuse this group of people with illegal immigrants, the better the chances of reducing racism and xenophobia*".

The ENEAS DP has also brought together stakeholders who had never had any form of structural cooperation before EQUAL. The collaboration agreements enabled the different actors to work together, share expertise and experience and identify effective solutions of benefit to all. As a result of their experience, most partners are keen to establish mechanisms for permanent cooperation.

Gaining valuable experience in the hospitality industry

Thanks to the training course, an asylum seeker from Colombia was not only able to upgrade his skills and get a qualification, but also to participate in an internship, which provided him with useful references. Gabriel explained the benefits he gained by stating that: *"The experience and qualification I gained by the end of the training programme opened the doors to getting an employment contract."*

A more detailed version and other EQUAL success stories can be found at: http://europa.eu.int/comm/employment_social/equal/activities/ search_en.cfm

Country: Spain (National coverage)
Project name: ENEAS
Project duration: May 2002 – December 2004
ESF priority area: Asylum seekers
ESF funding (€): 5 006 957
Total funding (€): 7 152 797
National EQUAL partners: Asociación Comisión Católica Española de Migraciones (ACCEM), Comision Española de Ayuda al Refugiado, Cruz Roja Española
Transnational partnership with: Austria, the Netherlands
Contact details:
Secretaria de Estado de Inmigración y Emigración
c/ José Abascal,4- 3ª planta
E-28003 Madrid
Tel: +34 915689451
E-mail: ramurrio@mtas.es, clarrec@mtas.es
Website: www.eneas-equal.org

Innovation

Mainstreaming

Transnationality ►

Empowerment

Partnership

Asylum seekers qualify to help others

Imagine you are in a country where you do not speak the language and you need to see a doctor. What would you do? Try to find someone who could accompany you and help translate? This could prove more difficult than it sounds. Medical terminology is not that easy and it may be very hard to explain the exact problem, not to mention understanding the doctor's response. Asylum seekers may also be traumatised and have difficulties expressing what the problem is, even in their own language. This is a situation many asylum seekers end up in when they arrive in a new country, and just one problem they face in access to social and healthcare services.

Knowing the language is just the starting point for integrating in a new society and finding work. For many asylum seekers getting a job is extremely difficult, since language is not the only obstacle they face. There may also be strict requirements for obtaining a work permit, as in Germany.

The TransSPuk Development Partnership, led by the Regional Office Berg City Triangle Remscheid Solingen Wuppertal, has established a new profession by creating a qualification for asylum seekers to become language and cultural mediators in the public health and social services sectors. In Germany, there is an urgent need for this type of work. According to a study at Berlin Charité hospital, just 1% of asylum seeker patients had access to professional interpretation. In other cases patients had to make themselves understood with the help of relatives – often children – or support staff, like cleaners. This can result in low quality of treatment of patients from migrant backgrounds, 'doctor shopping' and in the long run, increasing costs in the health care system.

Gaining a qualification, improving integration

The new profession of "cultural and language mediator", combining specific skills and language knowledge, paves the way for asylum seekers to gain a qualification while contributing to their new society and assisting other asylum seekers.

Asylum seekers are perfectly placed to do the job because of their rich linguistic and cultural backgrounds. By creating a qualification in which they learn about the social system and other features of German society, TransSPuk found an excellent way to improve asylum seekers'

chances of getting a job and integrating in their host country. At the same time it serves to enhance efficiency and decrease costs in the health and social service sectors.

The qualification developed by TransSPuk starts with two years' class-room education, followed by a one-year internship. Asylum seekers learn about Germany's social system and administration, cultural differences, computing and the German language. The practical training consists of internships in at least four different work environments, such as social and welfare services, clinics and hospitals. The final certificate they gain is of use not only in Germany, but also in case they return to their home countries.

Opening up to new cultures

The project has resulted in an increased awareness of asylum seekers and their needs. Both asylum seekers and staff got to know new cultures and the institutions became more open to other cultures and concepts. In fact, the various employers where asylum seekers undertook internships deemed the project so successful that they are now pushing for others to participate.

Varinia Morales of TransSPuk says "A lot of time has been invested in the project, but the outcomes have been great – once the ball got rolling a lot of positive things came out of it. For instance institutions and communes where asylum seekers completed internships started networking on their own initiative because they found the project so important. Partners who were initially sceptical about the benefits of the project became increasingly enthusiastic as progress was made, and actively promoted the DP."

The 27 asylum seekers who participated in the programme had very different cultural as well as educational backgrounds. Most were from crisis regions and came to Germany with very traumatic experiences. The majority were highly educated and had worked as teachers, architects, economists and engineers in their home country before they fled to Germany. Being able to get involved and do something useful helped them regain self-esteem and self-respect.

During the on-the-job training, over 60 internships were completed in 18 municipalities throughout the North Rhine-Westphalia region. The responses to job placements were overwhelmingly positive: the cultural and language mediators are now being used in over 140 different social and healthcare organisations, and have so far taken care of more than 1 300 cases. In 50% of cases, concrete job offers have been put on the table.

Results at national and European level

The university clinic of Hamburg Eppendorf has acknowledged and is certifying the job profile and the DP is now concentrating its efforts on obtaining national vocational recognition in the second round of EQUAL.

While the legal situation for asylum seekers in Europe varies from country to country, they all face the common problem of integrating into new societies, often with minimal or no support and guidance. TransSPuk came together with six other EQUAL Development Partnerships to form a transnational partnership called Asycult. Although the partner organisations come from different countries they all share the common goal of developing new education, training and supporting tools to improve asylum seekers' integration into their new society.

A more detailed version and other EQUAL success stories can be found at: http://europa.eu.int/comm/employment_social/equal/activities/ search_en.cfm

First day on the job

Country: Germany
Region: North Rhine-Westphalia
Project name: TransSpuk – Transfer von Sprache und Kultur in Gesundheits- und Sozialversorgung
Project duration: January 2002 – June 2005
ESF priority area: Asylum seekers
ESF funding (€): 1 009 923
Total funding (€): 2 091 993
National EQUAL partners: BSH mbH, Diakonie Elberfeld, Regionale Arbeitsstellen zur Förderung von Kindern und Jugendlichen aus Zuwander, Rhein-Ruhr-Institut an der Merkator-Universität Duisburg, Stadt Neuss, Ver.di
Transnational partnership with: Belgium, Greece, Italy, Luxembourg, the Netherlands
Contact details:
Regionalbuero Bergisches Staedtedreieck
Gemarker Ufer 17
D-42275 Wuppertal
Website: www.transspuk.de
Or Diakonie Wuppertal
Varinia Morales
Ludwigstr. 22
D-42105 Wuppertal
Tel: +49 202 496970
E-mail: morales@migrationsdienst-wuppertal.de
Website: www.sprakum.de

European Commission

EQUAL Success Stories – Development Partnerships working against discrimination and inequality in Europe

Luxembourg: Office for Official Publications of the European Communities

2005 – 65 pp. – 21 x 29.7 cm

ISBN 92-79-00180-9